SERMONS

ON THE

FAILURE OF PROTESTANTISM,

AND ON

CATHOLICITY.

BY THE

REV. FERDINAND C. EWER, S. T. D.,
RECTOR OF CHRIST CHURCH, NEW YORK.

NEW YORK:
D. APPLETON AND COMPANY,
90, 92 & 94 GRAND STREET.
1869.

CORRESPONDENCE.

NEW YORK, *November* 19, 1868.

REV. F. C. EWER, D. D.:

BELOVED RECTOR,—The undersigned, Wardens and Vestrymen of Christ Church, respectfully request the manuscripts of your late able sermons on "The Failure of Protestantism" for publication; believing, as they do, that the wide spreading of the same will prove a great benefit to the Catholic cause in the Church.

Very respectfully yours,

(Signed) SPENCER K. GREEN, *Senior Warden.*
JAMES DIXON, *Junior Warden.*
JOHN H. RUCKEL,
HENRY A. WILMERDING,
JAÇOB LANSING,
CHARLES T. COOK,
GEORGE H. PERINE, } *Vestrymen.*

REPLY.

CHRIST CHURCH RECTORY,
NEW YORK, *November* 20, 1868.

DEAR BRETHREN: Your note of yesterday is before me. I beg you will accept my thanks for its kind expressions. Arrangements, however, are already closed with the Messrs. Appleton, who have the sermons you allude to in hand for publication; otherwise they would be freely at your disposal.

Very truly your friend and rector,

F. C. EWER.

To Messrs. GREEN, DIXON, RUCKEL,
and others, of the Vestry.

NOTE.

Inasmuch as the following Sermons were written to be preached before mixed congregations, the reader will therefore pardon such repetition of ideas as he may observe.

F. C. E.

Christ Church Rectory, N. Y.,
St. Andrew's Day, 1868.

CONTENTS.

SERMON VII.

SERMON VIII.

SERMONS.

I.

FAILURE OF PROTESTANTISM.

"I came not to send peace but a sword."—St. Matt., x. 34.

The history of Christianity illustrates this text. Her career has been marked by crises, when men, stirred by unusual earnestness, have risen against the quiet order of things round about them. These crises have occurred at irregular intervals. They have always been provoked by some evil that has been long and silently growing. They are periods which try men's souls, because they are periods when new men attack old and cherished prejudices. In the second century after Christ the germs of what afterward became Arianism appeared in Lucian of Antioch. Those germs grew and spread in the Church silently, but so widely and alarmingly at last, as to lead earnest Catholics in the subsequent century to rise in their majesty, reassert the Faith in its purity as it had come down from the Apostles, and brand the new dogmas as deadly heresy. In the Middle Ages Roman errors silently and slowly grew and spread, till at last, in the eleventh century, earnest Catholics in the Eastern portion of the Church, enduring the evil no longer, rose in their majesty to condemn it; and that non-intercommunion with Rome was decreed by the Orthodox Eastern (or Greek) Church, which has lasted till to-day. In the Roman portion of the Church the same evils continued to grow, with new ones which broke out from time to time, until at last, in the sixteenth century, earnest men all over the West rose in their majesty against them; and we have the Reformation—so called. Subsequently coldness and deadness grew and spread in the Anglican portion of the Church, till at last, in the eighteenth century, those earnest souls, John and Charles Wesley, kindled the blaze of Methodism. God hath cast our lines at the opening of one of these crises. I would not have you unalive to the fact, or undervalue its importance.

For many years men have been floating calmly down the stream of Christianity. There have been petty differences and discussions between sects, it is true, but no general upheaval. Foundations have been undisturbed. But now a storm is very evidently rising which is disturbing the bottom of affairs; and it is impossible to predict how we shall all come out of it. There are evils raising great fronts around us, evils that have been long and silently growing. And as in the fourth century, as in the eleventh, as in the fifteenth, and as in the eighteenth, earnest souls are at last roused at these evils, and men are beginning boldly to speak out. It is noteworthy that the laity are ahead of the clergy in this matter. It is the evident and disastrous failure of Protestantism as a religious system, first, to reach the masses, and secondly, to preserve Christianity on earth, that is raising the mutterings of this storm. What is it that is the mother of all this infidelity? What is it that is the prolific cause of all this low grade of spirituality in character and life? What is it that hath broken up respect for old age, for parents, for authorities? What is it that hath laid Christianity open to the successful attacks of any resolute skeptic? What is it that hath dimmed the clearness of the eye of faith? What is it that hath removed the spiritual world and its dwellers far off to an astronomical distance, practically sundering the communion of the saints by the wall of death? What is it that hath substituted sentiment for principle—that standeth over the sick-bed anxious to wrest from the lips of the sufferer a cabalistic—a magical utterance about belief in Christ, that shall save him *in* his sins, but with scarce a word as to repentance and confession and amendment, and his salvation *from* sin? What is it that is the prolific cause of all this absence of the self-sacrificing spirit? What is it that has left the masses without a religion, and that has set us all on a course where we are at last ignorant as to how we can get at those masses? Mission Chapels for the poor, with Protestant or semi-Protestant services, and with a limited attendance at each of the well-to-do poor, are amiable but melancholy efforts of the day. God knows we are thankful for the good they do, but it is time that we no longer flattered ourselves that with them we are getting at the masses. The very pamphlets on church work that are pouring from the press are indications that we are walking in darkness; that we have been and are in the midst of some great blunder. What is it that hath set its face stubbornly, and reared stubborn prejudices against the only appliances that have ever succeeded in reaching down to the masses so as to hold them under control? It is time for us to ask how much the Protestant prejudices, which we have inherited from generations behind us by no means infallible, are worth, and how much they are costing. It is time for us to ask whether we shall longer weigh them against the Christianizing of millions of the neglected poor. What is it that hath left ministers stranded upon the high rocks of life, preaching to the select rich? What is it that hath sold the gospel to the rich in the house of God? What is it that hath hushed the voice of resounding praise throughout the great congregation, and delegated the praise of God to a salaried four? What is it that hath killed out from among us all anxiety for the salvation of God's MAN, as a unit of creation, extending through all time and space on earth, and that has elevated instead that selfish aspect of religion which makes it simply a process for the salvation of the given individual? Your and my salvation, my brother, are, of course, all-important to ourselves; but God, when He made His Church, made it for all time and for MAN, in the fullest meaning of the word. Nowadays, however, so long as a given individual of to-day can "get saved" in some human religious institution, that institution is considered as answering all the purposes of the Church; and there is not the slightest anxiety as to whether or not that institution contain a theological disease which will kill it, and leave the individual of two centuries hence without any institution to "get saved in."

I propose to call your attention to a few of the facts that mark the disastrous failure of Protestantism; and to ask you whether those facts are not enough of themselves—to say nothing of others—to stir to its depths any spirit that has a particle of earnestness. And I warn you beforehand, that, if Protestantism has failed, we are not to look to Rome for a cure. A recent able writer * has said, this would be but to fly from the effect to the cause. Justly has he said it; for Protestantism was produced by the errors of Rome; and why fly for cure from a system that has proved itself

* The Rev. Dr. M. Dix.

false in the nineteenth century to one that proved itself false in the fifteenth?

I remark, first, that in this city there are 300 churches—some of them large—most of them comparatively small. They will hold, when all full, say about 200,000 persons—call it 250,000. Where are the other three-quarters of a million of people in this city every Sunday? Making a liberal allowance for children too young to attend, for the sick who cannot, and for all engaged in employments for the public convenience, and considering those of our vast floating population who attend as strangers, and considering, moreover, the empty seats in all the churches each Sunday, there is an enormous residue that are non-church-goers. Compare, nay, contrast the immense church-attendance of the population in Roman and Greek Catholic countries with the attendance of the mere fragment of the population in Protestant lands. My friends, have you ever thought of the fact that there are countless thousands all over this land, that have *rejected* Protestantism? Have you ever thought of the fact that Germany has, as a nation, rejected Protestantism? Look, too, at New England, the headquarters of Infidelity in America. Look, too, at the Protestant Cantons of Switzerland. I do not mean to say that, in rejecting Protestantism, these countless thousands have taken to Rome; but they have at any rate abandoned the Protestant presentment of Christianity. There is scarcely a man or a woman in the land that has not a relative—shall I not say relatives?—who, while they still have a kind of respect for the Christian religion, no longer believe those dogmas that all Protestant denominations preach in common. The fact is, with the most of them, dogmatic Christianity is identified with its Protestant presentment. They know no other; and, in abandoning Christianity for skepticism, it is Protestantism that they have weighed in the balances and found wanting. And there are thousands of men and women, therefore, that at last do not go to church anywhere. These men and women are rearing children; and the latter are, by example, by casual domestic remark, and by carelessness of their parents, inheriting a similar abandonment. Protestantism has been trying to meet the evil by modifying and softening some of its subordinate dogmas. But people see that its fundamental dogmas remain, and that the modified subordinate dogmas only make the whole system more thoroughly inconsistent with itself; and so the great evil of abandonment grows greater and greater.

Now rise a grade above this class, and take the men and women that do attend church. How many of them are there that really believe Christianity as presented by Protestantism? Some of its dogmas they believe from habit, from early prejudice, or they scarcely know why. But those whose minds are shaken as to the rest form a very large element of every Protestant congregation.

This is a fact which the clergy may not wish to contemplate. But it is a fact. Here we see not total abandonment, but that process of abandonment in progress, which has been working for much more than a century, and which is at last very noticeable from the large proportions it has at length assumed. These two classes I have mentioned form the vast bulk of the community. Isn't that an alarming fact? What are you going to do with your prejudices against Catholicity under the circumstances? Mark me; I make a sharp distinction between Catholicity and Romanism. Now turn and look at the individuals that compose these two classes. There was a time when it was the staple remark that men became infidels because they desired to live a wicked or careless life. Doubtless there are some even to-day who are skeptics for the above-mentioned reason. But it were sheer blindness thus to account for the present general disease of infidelity which afflicts the community. Look around upon our relatives and friends who belong to the two great classes I have spoken of. Are they bad men? No. Are they unreasoning or unreasonable men? No. Are they unearnest men? No. Many of them are filled with the spirit of honesty, and truthfulness, and uprightness, and conscientiousness, and nobleness, and generosity, and hospitality, and kindness of heart, filled with all that which is the very basis of religion. Often they are men that stir our admiration for their good qualities of mind, and heart, and conscience. But they are logical men —men who cannot be stayed from passing into the legitimate conclusions that follow from false premises; and they have, therefore, consciously and conscientiously rejected (that is the word, *rejected*), either in whole or in part, the Protestant presentment of Christianity, and deliberately remain in their rejection. The grandfathers were Calvinistic Presbyterians, the fathers were Congregationalists, the sons were Unitarians, the grandsons are Parkerites and infidels. The attempt to mend Protestantism as a religious system ends in abandoning it altogether as a hopeless case. The Rationalists have a ground to stand on; the true Catholics have a ground to stand on; but Protestantism has no *locus standi* (if I may use such a phrase), and its process of disappearing I have given above. The men I speak of either do not think of or do not care to accept Rome, and so they are left without any distinctive religion, unless we can say, indeed, that each has his own.

The two basis ideas of Protestantism are, first, "the Bible, and the Bible only for Christians;" secondly, "each man practically his own infallible interpreter of it." Now, the consequence of this is, that Protestantism has not fostered humility, but arrogance. It has not cast over the individual mind the wholesome shadow of a distrust in its own ignorance, or partial views, or unexamined prejudices; but it has spread broadcast the rampant spirit of practical individual infallibility. And so these men, nursed in that school, absorbing the spirit from the very atmosphere about them, are perfectly satisfied, unalarmed, and at peace, each in his own partial or complete infidelity. Then, again, they see how these two basis ideas have led to the thousand conflicting sects of Protestantism, the splitting up of denominations on little petty points which their common sense tells them are unimportant; and so they gladly escape the maze in disgust, and, with a self-complacent down-looking upon the whole field of battling Protestant sects, settle down themselves into the mere religion of being good men. It is all very well, it is praiseworthy, this being a good man; but it isn't Christianity. And so far as all these men are concerned, Jesus Christ was incarnate, died, rose, established His Church and endowed it with His life-nurturing Sacraments in vain. So far as these men are concerned, God inspired the Bible in vain; for they reject it. They will take parts of the Bible and say they are true; but it is because those parts appeal to their minds as true. That is to say, Protestantism has wrecked the community on the rocks of individualism, and left each man to be a Bible to himself. Some people say, "Any good man is a Christian." But there were good men and true and honest before Christ came, millions of them. Ancient civilizations could not have existed; indeed, no civilization can exist without an enormous leaven of such elements. But the phrase "any good man is a Christian," and the phrase "a true Christian is a good man," are by no means identical. A good man is not necessarily a Christian. A true Christian is a good man, of course; but he is a good man who accepts the Bible and all its truths and commands, who accepts the incarnate Christ as his Saviour, and the Blessed Sacraments as the instrumental means of salvation appointed and commanded by Christ.

Now, what is it that has led to and is responsible for the rise of these two enormous classes in the community? My friends, it isn't Christianity as presented by the One Holy Catholic and Apostolic Church; for She has not yet got the ear of the people, and Her truths are moreover very much hushed even in Her own pulpits. Nay, it is the Protestant presentment of Christianity that has had their ear for the last two centuries. By its fruits shall ye know it. And this wholesale abandonment of it, that has been silently and steadily spreading in the last century, till it has invaded every family, is one of the indications of the failure of Protestantism as a system; and is arousing many reluctant but determined souls to the sad duty of dragging down that which has been quietly sitting on a throne as a king, too sacred to be touched, and solemnly arraigning it at the bar for trial. Protestantism, give us back our fathers, our children, our husbands, that are lost in the forests of skepticism! It is this that is arousing and banding together a broad Catholic party in the Church, which, if it will not close its eyes to the Roman failure of the fifteenth century (a failure made doubly disastrous by the Bull of 1854), is determined no longer to close its eyes to the Protestant failure of the nineteenth. A party that is determined to maintain and spread all that is truly Catholic that has come down from the past, and combine with it all of the present that has proved itself good, both in thought and in appliance. It is this that has provoked the beginnings of a second reformation, that will be a Reformation indeed; *Reformation*, did I say? RESTORATION is the better word.

In this claim that Protestantism has failed, you will not, of course, understand me as asserting that there was nothing good in the upheaval of the sixteenth century. This would be but mere extravagance, foolish exaggeration, and not the result of that calm, attentive out-look which the seriousness of the times and its dangers demand. That upheaval was as much in the interest of true Catholicity as it was in the interest of Protestantism. Nor will you understand me as meaning to say that, with all the enormous evils of the Protestant Heresy, there is nothing whatever that is good in it. Catholics are not unmindful that the Methodists, for instance, have struck something that is in harmony with human nature; and that that something can be wielded on the naturally enthusiastic heart of man in a better way, and on Christian rather than rationalistic plan. Make the man one with Christ through the sacramental system, and then bring in the lever of enthusiasm, and you have not substituted practical Immediation for Mediation, nor struck a ruinous blow at the foundation of Christianity. Catholics are not unmindful of Baptist practice or Unitarian literature. But I cannot pause upon this point.

I hasten to a second indication of the failure of Protestantism as a system. And I do so by asking the question: Protestantism, where are the masses? When we run our eye over the different sects, we are struck with the fact that each is made up of a peculiar type of man. There is, for instance, the Methodist type, and the denomination vary to greater or less extent around the type; then there is the Presbyterian type, and the Baptist, and the Quaker. I am not speaking disparagingly; far be it from me to do so. The whole matter is too serious. But we all know that men are constituted differently, and have different appearances. This is so nationally. No one would mistake a Frenchman for a Scotchman or for a German. This is so, too, inside of our people. So that, speaking generally, there are nice points by which men may be classified. Now, as a fact, Protestantism has been able in the past to draw to itself, at least for a while, only certain classes of men and women. And the patent fact remains that it has failed to attract man in all his conditions and kinds. Of course, I do not mean to charge against it that it has not Christianized the whole world. What I mean to say is, that it has failed to be a religion suited to every kind of even the Aryan man. There are men of æsthetic tastes; its cold and mean appearance repels them. There are men who want a positive faith; its shifting dogmas disgust them. There are holy women and self-sacrificing men who would gladly live a life of self-abnegation and high spirituality, who would gladly give themselves up as laymen and laywomen to a life of prayer and charity; it frowns upon Sisterhoods and Brotherhoods; it says to such, Get you gone from my doors, I have no place nor need for such as you; and it turns them back either into the world or to Rome. Christ's cause needs vast amounts of money all the time; it has fostered selfishness toward Christ, so that when the offertory-plate passes down its aisles it is considered that the act should be tolerated as an exception; and, if it passes too often, the offertory-plate is regarded as a positive intrusion. As a fact, after two hundred and forty years of trial with a fair field, even where, as in this country, it has been overwhelmingly in the ascendant, it has failed to reach the masses. It has failed, even though it has preached, in very loud tones too at times, all the terrors of hell-fire, and pictured by contrast all the gross splendors of a physical heaven. And it is this, too, that is stirring earnest men. Where are the masses? Why do your appliances fail to make permanent harvests among them? God's man, for whom He sent Christianity, includes not only the rich merchant, and the respectable retail dealer, and the well-dressed, well-to-do and thrifty artisan, with whom your meeting-houses are filled, but the great base of the community also, the ragged laborer and the squalid. Where are the latter in your pews and at your meetings? Where is your control over them? Politics gathers in all indiscriminately at its assemblages. How about Christianity? What is the matter with you? How long will you blindly hug your prejudices, and leave Rome to be the only one that can reach down to and control the masses? My friends, look at the Roman and the Greek branches of the Church, and contrast them with Protestantism in this respect. Why is it that the Anglican branch of the one great Catholic Church has no more succeeded with the masses than has Protestantism? Why is it that there is an Episcopal type of man? It is because we have run our Catholic and Apostolic wheels in the Protestant, Calvinistic, and Lutheran ruts, which they do not fit, never will, and never can. But wherever we have returned to, as in Holborn, London, and other places, and tried fairly our own true Catholic plan, we have, glory be to God, reached down to the masses, and gathered in all grades of men from highest to lowest. God is asking of Protestantism, Where are the masses? And God is saying to us, I gave you the ten Catholic talents; why have you hid them in a napkin?

It is not because the clergy and laity of Protestantism are unalive to the wants of the masses, or to their own duty in the premises, that Protestantism has made its signal failure. They are earnest and godly men. Heaven knows, they spare no efforts; instant in season, out of season, earnest in prayer and in work. But this only makes the matter worse. The fault is not in them. Men are often better than their systems, and, without doubt, the Protestant clergy and laity stand acquitted, while their system stands condemned.

I have mentioned but two counts in the presentment; time forbids me to go on with many others. But these alone, viz., first, the wholesale abandonment of Protestantism by large masses of thinking and good men, and, secondly, its failure to reach the masses, are signs of the times worthy of the thought of the churchman; and the two facts account, in some part, for a movement among us, which has not had its equal in earnestness and determination since the days of John Wesley; which is destined to lead to far more important results than his; a movement, my friends, which is deeper than ritualism, of which ritual is a mere fluttering red feather; a restating of the old Catholic and Apostolic grounds, free from admixture with Romish error; a returning to the old Catholic modes and appliances which belong to the Church as a reformed body, but which were torn out of Her one hundred years after She had reformed, and not by Her friends, but by Her enemies—Oliver Cromwell and his Roundheads, who broke into Her for that purpose; the scattered fragments of which the poor Church (when She rose from the prostrate and stunned condition in which Cromwell left Her) did not gather together for a while, and which have now been so long disused that we scarce know what they were. One thing we know: Our Church is a Catholic Church which has been worked on Protestant principles; and that something must be done. The masses must be reached, and this growing infidelity stopped by a more reasonable presentment of Christianity than Protestantism has succeeded in making, even by the widespread presentment of our true Catholic Christianity.

There is a school of thought in the Church which is "Broad" without the "Church." These would plunge us into rationalism. There is a school of thought that is "Church" without the "Broad." These would stiffen the Church into a fossil. But there is a school which is Catholic enough to hold to and get back all that has proved itself good in the past, and Broad enough not to hesitate to adopt all that has proved itself good in the present. This school is determined to hold up the Catholic Church in Her continuous life as God's Divine Institution, coming down with authority, and adapted to the wants of every man and of every century.

In a subsequent discourse I shall endeavor to answer the question, What is the Catholic Church?

II.

THE ANGLICAN CHURCH NOT PROTESTANT.

"The Pillar and Ground of the Truth."—1 Tim. iii. 15.

In accordance with the promise at the close of last Sunday's sermon, I am to speak to you of the Catholic Church. Two points are before me, viz.: first, to show briefly what the Catholic Church is; and secondly, to show that we are a part of that Church.

The word "Catholic" has its own, that is to say, its proper meaning. It has been used, in various languages, to convey this meaning, for eighteen hundred years. But there is an inclination among the sects to foist upon it a new meaning, not its own; to give it the meaning of "universal" in a certain vague sense, and then to say, "Oh, we are all Catholics." The fact is, it really expresses a large and glorious idea; Protestants know it, and therefore desire the word for their own. But it is doubtful whether the 270,000,000 of Catholics will permit the 74,000,000 of Protestants to change its meaning for their own purposes.* Depend upon it, that when a Protestant utters the language of the Catholic creed, and says, "I believe in the Holy Catholic Church," he does not mean what that phrase was written to mean, and has meant for centuries, and honestly means to-day. There is a mental reservation within him. But there is this comfort, namely: even though Protestants steal the name, they can never wipe out that mighty thing of which, since the opening of the Christian era, it has been the title.

However, when we leave names and come to things, we find persons even in the Church, who glory in that which is known under the term "Protestant." And such persons would triumphantly ask, "What! is not our Church 'Protestant?' Are we not the *Protestant* Episcopal Church?" In part reply to such I make this preliminary remark, viz., that the term "Protestant Episcopal" has never been formally adopted as a title for our Church. It is barely possible that I have overlooked the supposed fact of such adoption, but I hardly think it can be so. As nearly as I can find, the title stole in upon us like a thief in the night. What appears to be the history of the case? Why, the title of the Prayer-Book of the Church of England was, "The Book of Common Prayer, etc., of *The Church*, accord-

* The Roman Catholics number 170,000,000; the Greek Catholics, 80,000,000; and the Anglican Catholics, 20,000,000.

ing to the Use of the United Church of England and Ireland." That is to say, "The Prayer-Book of *The Church*—of *God's Church* in England." This title recognized that there was only One Church. Very well; before the Revolution it was the same in America. After the Revolution, it became necessary for the Church—for God's Church—to have a Prayer-Book suited to its wants in America as an independent nation. A general convention was held here. That convention expressly declared that, in whatever it did, it was "far from intending to depart from the Church of England in any essential point of doctrine." Now, that convention was an exceedingly small body; for the Church in America almost died during the Revolution. But, before the convention was held, several preliminary meetings of churchmen convened. The calls for these meetings were issued by irresponsible persons; and in those calls those private individuals—those irresponsible persons—designated the Church as the "Protestant Episcopal Church," as though God had a dozen other different kinds of Churches. It was their mere notion to call it so. Very naturally (considering the times) the same name, having thus been brought out, was used in all the subsequent letters that passed to and fro concerning the movement; and was continued in the summons for the first general convention. It was used by the few individual members of that convention in their speeches. It got into resolutions they offered, and into other documents that were adopted by the convention. It continued its stealthy advance, and got on to the title-page of the Ritual that was adopted. Who put it there? What printer, what private member of a committee, what unauthorized person? In vain have I searched the records of those early days, to find that the convention ever adopted the title-page to the Prayer-Book. Thus, it has secured a tacit sanction as a title, or rather, I should perhaps be more accurate in saying, a tacit *acceptance* as a title; but I repeat, it was never formally adopted as such by the Church here in her corporate capacity. The fact is, the question concerning a proper title for the Church never came up. The very utmost that can be said is, that the title has only had a mere *quasi* adoption. But the question *is* up now fairly and squarely; and it is for us to consider whether we ought longer tacitly to sanction the title by putting forth every new official document in the name of the "Protestant Episcopal" Church.

The name has wrought us untold harm and loss. It has falsified our position in the eyes of the public. It has identified us with those who hate our distinctive and vital peculiarities, our Apostolic succession, our non-recognition of man-made ministries, our non-reception of their "ordinance" of the Lord's Supper at their hands, our real presence of Christ in the Blessed Eucharist, our baptismal regeneration, our natural sympathies with the Greek Church, which they regard as only one step less vile and monstrous than Rome. It has fostered within us a Puritan, a strictly Protestant and un-Church sentiment, which has at last come out in a pink-covered pamphlet, asking whether there are not Catholic (the writer calls it "Romanizing") germs in the Prayer-Book; a pamphlet which admits that those who hold sound Church sentiments among us have, after all, been all along true to their Prayer-Book (the "precious" Prayer-Book of the Evangelicals), and true to their Church, and which proves in a most masterly way that, if the Prayer-Book is to suit the sentiments of the other, the so-called "Evangelical" party, it must be altered very materially.

Now, what is Protestantism, and what is Catholicity? Then, we shall be able to tell very easily whether our Church is Catholic or Protestant. Of course, I cannot answer these great questions in one discourse. I beg you to note, moreover, that it is not my present purpose to prove that the Catholic view is true; this would open up too wide a field; but merely to give a general idea of what Catholicity is as contrasted with Protestantism. The day is past for us longer to talk about "High Church" and "Low Church." The battle has widened out on to a larger field. The real struggle has larger scope. We have got to come up out of mere Anglicanism to the high standard of Catholicism. As Protestantism is mere incipient rationalism, the first duty of Catholicity is, to throttle it; we must clear the field first, that the grand, the only real struggle, may be set between Catholicity and rationalism itself.

Now, I desire to say this first, viz.: there are certain views held in the Roman Church which are not Catholic, that is to say, are not held by the Catholic Church; and yet Rome is a Catholic Church. This may seem a strange, perhaps a self-contradictory statement to you; but I hope to make it clear by-and-by. And there are certain views held in the Greek Church, and certain other views held by our Church, which are not Catholic; and yet the Greek and the Anglican are both Catholic Churches.

I remark, first, then, Protestantism founds the Church on the Bible, making the Bible prior. On the other hand, Catholicity rests the Bible on the Church, making the Church prior. Ask a Protestant which he believes first, Church or Bible? and he will say, "Bible." Ask him which he believes *because* of the other? and he will say, "I believe in a Church, because I believe in the Bible." "You start, then, with the Bible?" "Yes." "But how do you know the Bible is the Word of God?" "Why, I know it because 'All Scripture is given by inspiration of God.'" "But, my friend, the question is, *what is* Scripture? how do you know that these sixty-six books are the Scripture? Why is 'Solomon's Song' Scripture, and not the 'Book of Wisdom?' Why the 'Epistle of St. Jude,' and not the 'Epistle of St. Clement?' Where do you find in the Bible an inspired list of canonical books? And, if there were such list, how could you know that that list itself was inspired? If you fall back for aid on the holy Apostles, you find them quoting the 'Book of Enoch,' and displaying familiarity with 'Wisdom' and 'Ecclesiasticus,' and even quoting passages from the heathen poets." The Protestant has no answer; or he may take refuge in the remark that he believes the Bible on account of its evidences. "But have you ever personally examined those evidences to see if they are sound?" "No; but others have, and so, the Bible being generally accepted, I accept it." And after a series of questions, my brethren, you find it all comes to this, namely, that he believes the Bible to be the Infallible Word of God, on the testimony and assurance of fallible men. As another has expressed it, the world is put very comfortably on an elephant, and the elephant on a tortoise, but the poor tortoise rests nowhere. My friends, you may lay the Bible open, and you may scatter your open Bible till it is in every household, hotel, and steamboat; but for all that, if it rests nowhere, it will fall, as it has fallen in Germany, New England, and wherever Protestantism prevails. If Rome has been in error for closing the Bible (and there is no doubt but that She was in grievous error for so doing), did it ever strike you that She has nevertheless somehow succeeded in preserving a hearty, unreserved belief in it, and a reverence for it throughout her people, which Protestantism, with its Strausses and Parkers and Martineaus and Unitarians and hundreds of thousands of skeptics, has lamentably failed to do? An open Bible is indispensable for the world's good (there is no mistake about that), when your open Bible is tenderly cared for, and not thrown away, till people regard it as little worth. But many persons suppose that Protestantism and an open Bible are almost synonymous terms. Ah, but we must couple something else with the phrase "open Bible," if we would have it express the actual result of Protestantism round about us. That result is "an open Bible" indeed, but it is "an open Bible torn to pieces." We thank Protestantism for helping true Catholicity in England to open the Bible; we have no thanks for the rest she has done, and we will not close our eyes to it.

I do not mean to imply that there is no infidelity and no tampering with the Holy Bible in Roman Catholic lands. But I assert that such infidelity as there is in Roman lands has sprung out of the extravagances and the errors which Rome has superadded to her Catholic system. We equally oppose the Protestant heresy and the Roman alterations of Catholicity. Both have wrought vast evils upon the world. But I am not now treating Romanism, therefore I pass on.

Now, on the other hand, how is it with Catholicity? It rests the Bible on the Church. The Catholic knows the Bible is the Word of God, because the infallible Church tells him it is. But how does he know that the Church is infallible? I find, he replies, all round about me as a matter of notoriety, "a vast body existing in the world, professing to be the keeper, guardian, and interpreter of a book called the Bible." This body is not an abstract idea; it is an actuality in visible existence round about me. It has definite limits and visible peculiarities, so that I may recognize and know what and where it is. I trace this body from the present down through past centuries. I find it diminishing in size as I go back. I trace it continuously down and into the first century. I find it passing down deeper than the New Testament. I find it (earlier than the date of the New Testament) resting back into the holy apostles and Christ. And I find that they, upon whom the Church thus rests back as a basis, are surrounded by a glory of miracles and other positive attestations that they are from God, and act authoritatively. I find, in fact, that God was with them, nay, that God Himself came down and became man, to be—not the founder of something different and distinct from Himself, but the very Beginning and continuous Life of that Church, just as the individuality that is in the infant continues through and pervades its subsequent existence. I find that God, when He became man, and thus created the Church in and on Himself, and as an inseparable part of Himself, imparted to It the Truth, gave It authority to teach that Truth to all the world, and promised to continue with It till the end of time, guiding It infallibly. Thus I have the Church resting back, not on the New Testament, but resting back behind the New Testament, on no less than the Truth Incarnate Himself. If Christ is in and through the Church as Its very Life and Soul, then, of course, the Church cannot err. And if, on the other hand, the Church can err, then it cannot be that the Incarnate Truth Himself pervades Her. So you must either have an infallible Church, or a Church without Christ. And Protestantism can take either horn of the dilemma it likes. To have an infallible Church, I must have that on which She rests, and which ever after pervades Her, to be no less and no other than the Truth Incarnate. And, furthermore, I find myself forced to believe that Jesus Christ, who founded the Church, and promised to be with Her, was the Truth Incarnate, because I find, behind Him in time, a glorious series of prophecies that such a Being should come, converging toward Him out of long prior ages, and centring at last upon Him.

We do not reason in a circle. We do not prove the New Testament by the Church and then the Church by the New Testament. The Bible is a revelation of divine mysteries; but this visible Church—running back with continuous life behind the New Testament, and on to a basis which is itself surrounded by a glory of miracles, that basis resting upon long prior prophecy as a substructure—is an historic fact; and, if the Bible were to-day wiped out of existence, could be traced back like any other stupendous and patent fact in the world's career.

Now, during the first hundred years or more of the existence of this Church, many gospels and epistles were written to Her. And she, already in existence before them, and already having the promise that the Incarnate Truth who was in Her would guide Her infallibly, selects certain ones out of the multitude of documents written to Her, binds them into a New Testament, preserves them and hands them on to me as the infallible Word of God. Thus I have either an infallible Word of God, resting on an infallible Church, which itself, as an historic fact, rests on the Truth Incarnate, who surrounded Himself with a glory of miracles when He came, to give me notice that He had come, and to Whom a long series of prior supernatural events in the world's history pointed, or I have nothing under the sun that I can trust in as a Bible. The very infallibility of the Bible demands the infallibility of the Church; the two stand or fall together.

Now, beloved, the Church was to be the pillar and ground of the truth, the keeper of the Word, as an invaluable deposit for all time. Let us see, then, whether Protestantism is trustworthy in this respect; whether it has kept the Word. Are sacraments in the Bible, Baptism, the Holy Communion, Orders? Yes. Well, are Quakers Protestants? Yes. But they have given up sacraments. Protestantism has let a portion of the Word slip out, then, at that hole. Is Confirmation in the Bible? Yes? Well, are Presbyterians and Congregationalists and Baptists Protestants? Yes. But they do not believe in Confirmation, and do not practise it. Protestantism has let another portion slip out, then, at that hole. Is the Old Testament a part of the Bible? Yes. Are Unitarians Protestants? Yes. But Unitarians as a body think very little of the Old Testament; they have dropped it to all intents and purposes as an effete book; some of them more, some of them less of it. So Protestantism has let a portion slip out at that hole. Are the Parkerite-Unitarians Protestants? Yes. Well, are the Epistles a portion of God's infallible Word to us? Yes. But Parkerites say they are not. So Protestantism has let another portion slip out at that hole. Now take the balance of the Bible, namely, the four Gospels. Are they a part of God's Word to us? Yes. But is the Church up here on Fortieth Street Protestant? Yes; but its pastor writes and teaches in last August's magazine that the four Gospels are fables born of the heated and hero-worshipping imagination of centuries subsequent to Jesus; and that, as for the actual Jesus that lived, a true record of Him is hopelessly lost to history. So Protestantism has let a portion of the Bible, and the balance of it, slip out at that hole.

Now, on the other hand, does the Greek Church hold to the whole Bible? Yes. Does the Roman? Yes. Does the Anglican? Yes; and when Colenso rises to say the Word of God is not the Bible, but is somewhere scattered round in it, nobody can tell where, the Anglican Church rises in all its national parts and ejects him as a heretic. That, then, which is the pillar and ground of the truth, the keeper of the Bible, is Catholicity only. The Church, then, which the Protestant's Bible speaks to him of, cannot be his Protestantism, but must be that vast Organic Body he so much hates, of which the Greek, the Anglican, and the Roman are parts. That Church, according to promise, has not erred as a whole, however Its parts may each have errors of its own. And all that we want in the great Catholic movement of to-day is for the three parts mutually and lovingly to point out each other's errors, as they are beginning to do, and for each of the three to look candidly at its own; remembering that God has not promised infallibility to any one part, however large, any more than He has to any one individual, but only to the whole in their united, corporate and historic capacity. And that, therefore, any part, whether the Roman, the Greek, or the Anglican, when acting alone, is liable to err. And that no part—neither the Roman, the Greek nor the Anglican—has the right to set up its peculiar dogmas and impose them as Catholic truth on its sister parts. When the whole Catholic Church speaks again, then it will do for us to listen. Then we must listen. Now, as a whole, She has spoken in times past. She has spoken through Her six General Councils and their creeds. She stands in the past speaking to us through Her consenting voice touching the Eucharist, the doctrine of Baptism, the "other sacraments," as our Homily expresses it, and the glorious garments and stately forms that befit their administration. Protestantism cares nothing for all this—she hates it—she cares not for those General Councils. But see how the instinct of Catholicity bows humbly to them. And if you would test whether our Church is Protestant or Catholic, mark how She accepts the creed of those Councils, guards it as too sacred to be touched, makes her children repeat it often, and, when leaning over the deathbed, tells them that She will rehearse to them the articles of the Christian faith "that they may know whether they do believe as Christian men should or no."

I find that the subject is large, and that my time is rapidly passing, while I have but skirmished on the borders of the great topic. Should I take up a second point, it would prolong this discourse unduly. I must therefore postpone the second point, and beg to continue and close this sermon with a thought suggested by what I have said above. One of the ablest of our American clergy said, not long since (he did not express his thought in the same language, but it is substantially the same idea), that we have all of us been saying for years, "I believe in the Holy Catholic Church." But what have we been meaning all along? We have been meaning something very like this, viz.: I believe in the Holy Catholic Church—that is to say, from the year 33 to the year 100, *entirely*. I believe in the Holy Catholic Church from the year 100 to the year 600, *to a certain degree*. I believe in the Holy Catholic Church from the year 600 to the year 1500, *not at all*. I believe in the Holy Catholic Church from the year 1500 to the present time—that is to say, *in my portion of it*. But, beloved, that is not the Holy Catholic Church of your creed. We belong to a local Church; and we have been in the habit of calling the Anglican *the* Church, as though it were the whole. Just so Rome has called herself *the* Church, as though She were the whole; and the Greeks have called themselves *the* Church, as though they were the whole. But what is all this but the spirit of mere sectarianism broken out in the great Church Catholic, not the Catholic spirit? Let us combine with our friends, who are rising in Rome and in the East, for a great Catholic reformation, under which local errors shall be eliminated from each and every part. We have called each other hard names long enough. A family is an organic unit still, though the brothers are at sword's point; for God made the unity, and human passion cannot break it. We have tried hate for each other long enough. How much have we gained by calling Rome Anti-Christ, and how much has she gained by calling us heretics? It is high time we tried something else. Silence in the household, and peace! and let us see calmly what the matter is. The Catholic National Churches have a common basis of unity. Protestantism has none. And surely we have none with Protestantism. Of all places the Catholic Church is the last for the narrow, bigoted spirit of sectarianism. We, I say, belong to a local Church; but go up upon the hill-top and look out. Enlarge your view. There you shall see others—two hundred and fifty millions—differing with us, alas! in some things (but by no means hopelessly differing), but one with us substantially in the acceptance of that great creed, that great view of Christianity as a system, which is so different from the Protestant, and which has been set forth by the whole Catholic Church; one with us in owning allegiance to the same apostolically descended ministry; one with us in admitting the same idea of the Church as an organic Body united to the Lord, Her Head, by the same baptism, and fed with Him at the same altar. Remember that "Catholic" does not mean any part. That ministry only is Catholic which we all agree is the only authoritative, namely, the Apostolic; that faith only is Catholic which we all agree upon in common; every thing over and above is partial, local, and not Catholic. Those sacraments only are Catholic which all agree upon. Remember, then, that Rome, though *a* Catholic Church, is not *the* Catholic Church; and that we, though *a* Catholic, are not *the* Catholic Church. Remember that we must go deeper and broader to find the Catholic Church, down on to the great foundation where we all three stand; down out of the differences between the brothers and on to the unity of the family. Brethren, just there is the ground upon which we stand as Catholics; not as Romanists, not as Greeks, no longer as mere Anglicans, still less as local "Episcopalians," but in harmony with our great fundamentals, our ministry, our faith, and our sacraments, as Catholics. Remember that there is something more vast, longer in time, and larger in space, than the "Episcopal Church" so called; that our Church as a national body must be in subordination to the great authoritative Catholic Church—its views in subordination to Her greater views. Remember that only that doctrine is binding upon us all which the whole Church, with which the Lord promised to be, has set forth; and those practices and that ritual which are sympathetic, not with those who hate our fundamental principles, but, on the other hand, with whatever has been universal in the Church Catholic; and are sympathetic not with that mere intellectual presence of Christ which Protestantism upholds, but with that real and actual presence of Christ, which the Church has claimed and set forth to the world through all ages, and which the Lord Christ promised to His Church, and gave when He said, "This is my body."

III.

THE ANGLICAN CHURCH FUNDAMENTALLY DIFFERENT FROM THE PROTESTANT SECTS.

" The Church of the Living God."—1 Tim. iii. 15.

It is the popular impression that the Anglican Church took Her rise about three hundred years ago, in the days of King Henry the Eighth. She is believed to have been a creature of the Reformation, and is therefore regarded as one of the great sisterhood of the Protestant sects. She is looked upon as agreeing with those sects in all fundamental respects, and differing merely on subordinate points. It is supposed that, to a Protestant foundation, She merely superadds such matters of taste as written prayers instead of extemporaneous, the observance of certain festivals and fasts, the use of clerical garments, a preference for Gothic architecture, and for a ministry in the three orders of Bishop, Priest, and Deacon. To the inquiry, How the Church differs from the Protestant denominations about her? such points as the above-mentioned would be specified in reply. It is not at all imagined that fundamentally we are not with the Protestant, but with the great Catholic world. It is not at all imagined that the difference between us and all Protestant bodies is not superficial, but radical and irreconcilable.

But, Brethren, there are certain signs of the times that are very noteworthy. Why is it that, as the Protestant denominations are mutually drawing together, and seeking coalescence in union meetings and the interchange of pulpits, our Church stands aloof from the movement? Why is it, that if any of our Clergy, however few, coquet with the movement, the great body of our communicants, both lay and clerical, rise in indignation? Why is it, too, that, as this mutual gravitation is taking place among the systems of Protestantism, there is, on the other hand, a counter-movement springing up in each of the three great parts of the Catholic world—Greek, Anglican, and Roman—under which they are looking with kindlier eye upon each other, if not actually drawing into closer sympathy? That there are these two mighty clusterings it were folly to ignore. How shall we account for them? Is it not possible that, as the storm of the Reformation is subsiding, natural sympathies, springing out of fundamental agreement, are rising to resume their sway?

At any rate, here are two popular misapprehensions touching our Church, viz.:—first, as to Her origin, and secondly, as to Her position relatively to the Protestant denominations. It is to these two points that I shall direct my remarks this evening. In all fundamental respects our Church is neither recent, nor is She Protestant in the popular acceptation of that term. I do not, of course, deny that She protests against certain errors that have grown up in a territorial portion of the great Catholic body of which She is a part; but what I mainly propose to show is, not in what respect She differs from Rome, but in what respect She differs from all the Protestant denominations taken together: and, furthermore, to show that the difference between Her and them is so radical, that any compromise between the two is a logical impossibility.

In the last three hundred years theological matters have become confused by a mass of doctrinal detail; and it is not at all strange that, in the confusion, the ordinary mind should lose sight of the few main points that, after all, really cause us to part asunder. It is well, therefore, to withdraw at times into a calm distance where the details shall disappear from the vision, and the main distinctions come boldly out to view. Permit me, Beloved, for the sake of brevity, to call the system to which we adhere by the name under which it is known among us, viz., "The Church;" and to call the bodies collectively, who agree with us in so far as we protest against Romish errors, but who differ with us in so far as we Churchmen hold with Rome to the great underlying truths of the Catholic Church, by the title of "The Denominations," or "The Protestant Sects."

Before I proceed to our first head, namely, The Origin of the Church, let me ask you to recall sundry matters which are patent to the eye, in which the Church differs from the Denominations; for instance, the internal structure of our houses of worship, the arrangement of our chancels, so different from the ordinary Protestant plan of pulpit, with sofa behind and Communion-Table below, the constitution of our ministry in three orders, the fact that we have no revivals, etc. And to ask you whether all this, and more, ought not at least to raise a suspicion, before we commence, that there must be, underneath, some radical variance between the two systems. Can it be that two systems, so differing to the eye, are fundamentally at one with each other? Let us see. I proceed, then, to strike the clear, distinguishing note of the Church.

I. When did the Church arise? In order to see that She did not take Her origin at the same time with the sects, in the days of King Henry VIII., permit me to give a brief history of the Church Catholic from the first.

The Holy Apostles did not separate and go forth to plant the Church in all the world immediately after the Ascension of our Lord. The popular impression is that they did. But if you will turn to your New Testament, you will find that the Twelve remained residing at Jerusalem for twenty years after that event. During this period they preached to Jews, not to Gentiles. The Grecians spoken of in the sixth chapter of the Acts, were not Gentiles; they were Jews who spoke the Greek tongue. During this long period of twenty years, the adherents of Christ continued to be members of the Jewish Church, superadding Christian observances in their own gatherings. Meantime, a model form of the Christian Church grew up in Jerusalem under the combined hands of the Apostles, with Ministry, the Sacraments, the Faith, and a regular Form of Worship. The Liturgy was not committed to writing, but was memorized.

Some years after the Ascension, the conversion of St. Paul occurred; and it was toward the latter part of the above-mentioned period of twenty years, that he went forth into Asia Minor, and preached not only to Jews resident there, but also to Gentiles. This gathering of Gentiles as well as Jews into Christianity, precipitated a crisis, both in the action of the Apostles and in the career of the Church; for, in the new bodies of converts which St. Paul gathered, there speedily arose a contention. The Jewish converts insisted that the Gentile converts, in addition to their Christian duties, should comply with the requirements of the Mosaic ritual law. It was held that that law had been given in all its minutiæ by God Himself, and that all who believed in the true God must, of course, obey it. At last St. Paul goes down to Jerusalem, where the other Apostles were living, that this question (which, you will observe, was one of the gravest importance) might be settled by them. The Council of Jerusalem, an account of which is in the fifteenth chapter of the Acts, met, and decided the matter. The virtual conclusion reached was this, viz.: that the whole Jewish form of the Church had, after all, been fulfilled by the Life, Death, Resurrection, and Ascension of our Lord; that it no longer had any real existence; and that the Christian form of the Church had taken its place. This occurred about the year 50 or 52. Thus, it was not till twenty years after the Ascension that the Apostles, arousing to their newly-seen responsibilities, separated, and went forth to their great work of planting the Church Catholic in all the world.

The Church which they planted was identical everywhere, from Spain and England in the West, to Syria in the East;—identical in its Ministry, its Form of Government, its Sacraments, its Faith, and Liturgical mode of Worship. It is to be borne in mind that the Apostles, having once separated to this work, never afterward met together again for consultation. And yet such was the Church they planted. At the end of the first century, and in the beginning of the second, it rears itself everywhere before us as a vast visible body. Everywhere it has its Bishops, Priests, and Deacons; its Liturgies,* its Creed, its Chan-

* It should be noted that the Apostles did not leave only one

cels, its Altars, its Festivals and Fasts, and its Sacraments. Everywhere its Bishops are the only persons empowered to ordain to the Ministry. How happens it that the Apostles, who never afterward met together, should yet have planted a Church identical in every main point all over Europe, Civilized Asia, and Africa? The fact is, they each and all carried away in their minds the model form which had during the twenty years grown up under their combined hands in Jerusalem; and that they, each and all, planted the Church Catholic everywhere in general accordance with that model form.

But what, furthermore, was the condition of this Church Catholic? Everywhere it was One; but the Church in each nation was independent of the Church in any other nation; could ordain or discipline Her own clergy; could make Her own Canon Laws and arrange Her Liturgy in the vernacular of Her own people. When a man moved from Italy to Spain, or from Egypt to Greece or to England, he only moved out of one National Branch into another of the same Church Catholic. Thus like some vast banyan-tree the Church was one organism, but with an indepen-

form of Liturgy behind them in the Universal Church, nor yet twelve different forms; but, strange to say, four forms. These forms contained nearly identical parts, but differed in the arrangement of those parts; one arrangement prevailing in Syria and the East, the second in Egypt and Northeastern Africa, the third in Italy and Northwestern Africa, and the fourth in Asia Minor, Gaul, and Britain.

dent trunk in each country. Her condition was analogous, indeed, to that of the United States. Rhode Island, for instance, is independent of New York. It can make its own laws and elect its own officers without dictation from the Governor and Legislature of New York; and yet both States are a part of one Country. There are local peculiarities in each, but the same general characteristics.

Now, Apostles and apostolic men planted the Church Catholic in Rome, in Thessaly, in Gaul, in Egypt, in Britain. The National Branch of the Catholic Church planted in Britain in the first century was, in a certain sense, independent of the National Branch of the Church Catholic that was in Rome, and was its peer; less in wealth, less in influence, less in the mental ability of its Clergy perhaps, but endowed with the selfsame rights.* This mutual independence of the National parts of the Catholic Church lasted for centuries after the Apostolic days. But at last, about the seventh century, the National Branch

* When Gregory I., Bishop of Rome A. D. 596, sent Augustine to England, the latter sought to bring the British Bishops into subjection to the Bishop of Rome. A Conference was at length held, at which Dunod, a Bishop, speaking in behalf of his brethren, returned the following reply to St. Augustine, viz.: "We are bound to serve the Church of God; and the Bishop of Rome, and every godly Christian, as far as helping them in offices of love and charity; this service we are ready to pay; but more than this I do not know to be due to him or any other. We have a Primate of our own, who is to oversee us under God, and to keep us in the way of spiritual life."

of the Church in Rome began to usurp power over its neighbors in the West of Europe, to take away their independence, to fix its own laws, worship, customs, and officers upon them. Novel doctrines began also to grow up in Rome, superadding themselves to Her Catholic system. And in due time She spread those doctrines also through the National Branches She had subjugated. She threw Her yoke upon the Catholic Church in England. She tried to throw Her yoke also upon the numerous National Branches in the Eastern part of Europe; but never succeeded in this attempt. In England, however, as I have said, after a brave struggle on the part of the British Bishops, She succeeded; and for several centuries the Catholic Church in England, though of right independent, autonomic, was in the same position under Rome that Rhode Island would be, if for a while its large, wealthy, and powerful neighbor, New York, should reduce it to dependency, give it its laws, its judges, and other officers.

But in Henry the Eighth's time the National Branch of the Catholic Church in England succeeded in throwing off the yoke of Rome, and stood once more independent, reinstated in Her original position, rehabilitated with the rights which, a few centuries before, She had lost. It is immaterial whether the motives of Henry were conscientious or not; God maketh the wrath of the wicked to praise Him, and Henry's quarrel with Clement was the subjugated Church's opportunity in England.

Using Her regained rights, Her clergy and laity pruned and translated Her liturgy, reformed Her customs, and abolished from Her the novel and Romish doctrines that had been temporarily added to Her Catholic system. She remained still the same old National Branch of the Church that had come down in England from the Apostles' days; She had simply removed from Her Catholic structure the incrustations of Romish errors. Suppose a free man had, at one period of his life, been enslaved by a powerful neighbor, and had subsequently thrown off the yoke, why one might as well say that that man is not the same individual through it all, but that he only began to exist from the moment he regained his freedom, as to say that the Catholic Church in England took the origin of Her existence at the time of Henry the Eighth.

Understand, that it is one thing utterly to destroy the National Branch of the Church Catholic in a country and construct a new Christian organism in its place; but it is another and a very different thing to take the same old Church Catholic that is found in a nation, and merely remove from it such novel doctrines and improper customs as may have grown up within it, or been forced upon it. The former is what was done on the Continent; the latter is what was done in England. Thus the Continental and the English Reformations were conducted on a different principle each from the other. The one was destructive of Catholic truth and the Catholic Church, the other was preservative of both.

In the old colonial times of our country, the English branch of the old Catholic Church, acting according to the law of Catholic growth, put forth a branch into this country. And when, as the result of the American Revolution, England and America became independent nations, the Church in this country became, *ipso facto*, a national and independent trunk of the one Catholic Church in all the world.

Alas, that the fifteen or twenty gentlemen who met in the general convention immediately after the Revolution, and at the opening of the independence of the American Catholic Church, should have left us as a heritage that unfortunate title "Protestant Episcopal." For, what does the word "Protestant" indicate to the popular mind? Why, in general terms, a violent opposition to all that is Catholic. The word does not express, therefore, our attitude. For we adhere to, we cherish with undying fondness, much that is in the Romish Church which Protestantism hates and has abolished. We simply protest against certain of Her features, so that the title "Protestant," as applied to us, does not mean the same as when applied to the Denominations, and the popular mind is misled in regard to us. Again, the term "Episcopal" simply refers to our Church

Government. Thus the whole title, "Protestant Episcopal," selects only two out of very many of our characteristics (and those two by no means the most important), and elevates them into the prominence of an exhaustive designation for the whole. Why, brethren, you might as well call New York an "Anti-Mormon Gubernatorial State," and fancy that you have thoroughly defined your Commonwealth, as to dream for an instant that the title "Protestant Episcopal" is, ever was, or ever could be, a befitting name for the great American fraction of the One Holy Catholic Church in all the world. But, thank God, the fifteen or twenty wise gentlemen who, in the eighteenth century, took such action as has resulted in foisting this heritage of "Protestant Episcopal" as a title upon nearly forty vast dioceses in the nineteenth century, were not permitted by the Catholic Church elsewhere to carry out their intentions of laying violent hands upon the Creed itself. Thank God that that Creed does not read, "I believe in the Holy P. E. Church of the U. S. A." Thank God that it still reads as of old, "I believe One Catholic and Apostolic Church. I acknowledge one Baptism for the remission of sins; and I look for the Resurrection of the dead, and the Life of the world to come."

Thus the English Catholic Church, known as the Church of England, did not with the sects take Her origin in the Reformation. She merely succeeded in disenthralling herself at that stormy period. She is an ancient Branch of the Church Catholic, having a continuous life running down from the apostolic days to the present time; preserving, all along, Catholic features of the Apostolic Church visible, Her Ministry, Her Faith, Her Sacraments, Her Seasons, Her Liturgical Worship; free during the first six centuries, then enslaved by Rome for a while, then striking for and regaining her freedom again, which She has enjoyed now for the last three centuries. She still agrees with the Roman, the Greek, the Armenian, and other parts of the Church in all fundamental Catholic respects, and differs from the Roman part in respect of certain errors, which added themselves to Her Catholic system in the latter part of the middle ages and in the year 1854.

Thus the Church, instead of being fundamentally Protestant, that is to say, constructed on Protestant notions, and merely bearing a little about Her on Her surface that looks like the "visible," the "priestly," the "Sacramental," and the "Catholic," is, on the other hand, fundamentally, and has been continuously, Catholic, while such Protestantism as She has is a temporary expression, which She has been forced to put on at this period of Her long career, in censure of errors into which a portion (numerically a half, perhaps) of the great Body of which She is a part has fallen, as She trusts only temporarily. Thus you will see that, after all, the cause and the main object of Her existence is not to protest against those temporary errors (although she does that by the way), but it is the rather to continue to hold and to spread, as formerly, so now and to all future time, the great principles of the Church Visible, of Catholic Truth and Apostolic Order.

She belongs to the great Catholic Sisterhood. One erring sister has brought grief to the household. But She looks upon that sister, and, as She marks the familiar lineaments of the family, She cannot hate her; She grieves over the errors. She looks within herself, and finds that all is not perfect even there; She prays for her prodigal Sister, and She is beginning to pray for herself also. Far be it from Her ever to abandon the family of which She is a member, and take up Her portion beneath the fleeting tents of a hard, a hostile, and a wayward tribe! God speed the day when all the fair Sisters, Greek, Roman, Armenian, English, Russian, and American, shall abandon such mistakes as either may have fallen into, shall learn that no fraction can be the whole body, and shall stand, with arms intertwined, a one harmonious Catholic family once more!

When the two great clusterings, Protestant and Catholic, shall have completed themselves, the one organic like an army, the other disintegrated like a mob, and the shock between the two shall take place, can any one doubt the issue?

II. I come now to the second point, viz.: The Anglican Church being regarded by the popular mind as fundamentally one of the Protestant sects. Let me recall to you what I said above, namely: that it is my object to set forth wherein it is that the Church differs in fundamental doctrine from all the Denominations taken together. Is there the radical difference I speak of? If so, does it lie in the mere question of written or extemporaneous prayers, of baptism by pouring or by submersion, of whether or not it is Scriptural to baptize infants, of Church Government? Oh no. These are all questions of some importance, but they are superficial in the comparison. Can we or can we not go down beneath these to some one point where, to start with, the difference between the Church and the sects is so radical, that, after all, any subsequent compromise between the two is a delusion and a snare to both? If there be such a point, the plain man, who has little or no time to study into numerous and nice superficial theological distinctions, would like, of course, to know what it is, that he may be settled in his main religious position. All these differences between the Church and the Denominations which are apparent to the eye, for instance, as to Church Government, forms of worship, observance or non-observance of Feasts and Fasts, Infant Baptism, etc., are, if I may so express it, bewildering branches and twigs, in which the plain man finds himself entangled. My point is, that these branches and twigs, in fact all the peculiarities of the Church, spring out of the answer to a prior question. If that question be decided one way, we are carried into the entire Churchly set of branches in doctrine and practice; if the other way, we are carried into the Protestant set of branches. Surely it is an important point gained toward clearing up the complicated matter to our minds, and virtually disposing of a hundred-and-one subordinate questions, if we can go down from the branches to the two great trunks, the Churchly and the Protestant, and then get back to the root, and see, if possible, exactly where and why it is that the two great trunks themselves part company.

Now, the great question, which in itself alone divides us from all Protestant sects, is the all-important question, What is Election? This lies down under the surface; but this is it. And as we give one or the other answer to this question, What is Election? so do we consistently decide one or the other way on all subsequent questions.

Now, the Protestant idea is that Election is of individuals directly to life eternal. Thus with Protestants "the elect are identical with the finally saved." Protestant Denominations may differ among themselves as to the extent of Election, as to the limitation or universality of the Atonement as a potential means of salvation; they may differ as to the distinctness of the boundaries between the elect and all others; they may differ very much as to the *causality* of Election in the Divine Mind, that is to say, whether persons are elected by God's absolute and irrespective sovereignty, or whether (as the Methodists say) their election was, so to speak, influenced in the Divine Mind by their foreseen personal actions as free beings (God's Foreknowledge not affecting their acts, any more than one man's observing another's falling causes his fall); they may differ as to whether God has reprobated the non-elect or not; but they all agree as to the *ideality* of election; that is to say, that it is of individuals, and that its immediate design is eternal life. And if you would test this, ask any Methodist, or Calvinistic Baptist, or Free-Will Baptist, or Orthodox Congregationalist, or Presbyterian (New School or Old School, Supra-lapsarian or Sub-lapsarian), "Will any of the elect be lost and damned?" And, unless I mistake very much, they will one and all say, "No! It were dreadful to imagine such a thing for an instant!"

But the view of the Church, as expressed in Her prayers and offices, and homilies, and in Her XVIIth Article, is radically different from all this. And Her view gives to Her whole theology a different character. By reflex light it shines back upon Christ and upon God, and shows Them under a very different aspect to the world. It gives to Her whole presentment of Christianity a different cast, and it leads Her into a vastly different treatment of the sinner. Do you ask why it is that we have no revivals? The answer is, because of our view of Election; they are foreign to our whole system; nay, destructive of it. Do you ask, Why we baptize infants? The answer is, because of our view of Election. Do you ask, Why we have a ministry in three orders, Why we have a ritualistic form of worship, Why our Altars and not our pulpits are the prominent objects in our churches? The answer is, because of our view of Election. What is that view? I will give it to you.

The Church holds that "Christ came to introduce a new state of things on earth, a Kingdom of God; that He came not merely to found a religion; not merely to make an Atonement for individual sinners, but to establish a Kingdom of which He was to be the King. And it was to be more than a Kingdom. It was to be the Church; a company of men not only believing in Him but also baptized into His Body. And these persons, so blessed, were not merely to be under Him as their King, or instructed by Him as their Prophet, or reconciled through Him as their Priest, or individually to apprehend Him as their Sacrifice; but over and above all these things they were to be supernaturally joined to Him by a union so intimate, so entire and real, that it could only be illustrated by the union that subsists between the limbs of a human body and its head, or between a vine and the branches that form a part of it;" *

* The writer has taken liberties with the above extract from Sadler, in the way of adding to the language for greater fulness of expression, not in the way of altering the sense.

a union, I say, which, though supernatural, is yet real and not merely abstract; a union not like that which subsists between two consenting friends, but rather analogous to that which subsists between Adam and all who have derived their nature from him. So that Christ's Body Natural grows out, as it were, by the addition of those who are thus made one with Him, and becomes His Body Mystical. Christ and His Church Catholic are all one; we are the branches and He is the whole Vine. Christ is that Stone, spoken of by Daniel, "Cut out without hands . . . . that became a great mountain and filled the whole earth." The Church holds that the means by which God unites separate men to this great Body Mystical of Christ, so that they are buried in Christ, is Baptism.* Baptism is with Her no mere form, but an amazing reality. She holds, therefore, that Election is into the Body Mystical, is into high ecclesiastical privileges on earth, which, if they are used rightly, will enable a man to reach life eternal hereafter; but which,

* The Holy Spirit, on the Day of Pentecost, fell not on individuals *as such*, but on the Body of the Church. This indwelling presence of the Holy Spirit makes the Church something different from a mere company of men; makes It to be an object of faith. "We do not simply believe that there are persons who call themselves Christians; this is a fact which even the heathen know. We believe beyond this that all members of the Holy Catholic Church are joined together in one unseen Body by the Presence of the Holy Ghost," this Body being one with Christ, being His own Body Mystical.

on the other hand, if they are not used rightly, will not insure him salvation. While, therefore, the Protestant idea is that the elect are identical with the *finally saved*, the Church's idea is that "the elect are identical with *the baptized;*" that Election has, therefore, only mediate and not immediate reference to everlasting salvation, since some of the Baptized will be saved and some will not.

For we claim that God's great Church is one and continuous, not merely from Christ, but from the Fall itself down to the present time; that it was first Patriarchal in form, then Jewish, and finally Christian; that the scheme of Election (if I may be permitted to use such a phrase) was adopted at the Call of Abraham; that the Jews were God's elect people, some of them making their calling and election sure by using their high ecclesiastical privileges and helps aright, while others failed to do so, and failed, therefore, of the ultimate though not immediate end of their election. We claim that, when God changed the form of His Church visible, from Jewish to Christian, from National to Catholic, He did not change His idea of Election. The Aaronic ministry was changed to the Apostolic; the bloody features of the Church's Altar were stricken out, leaving only the bread and wine,* "the meat-offering and the

* The altar became a new power under the hand of Christ, for He gave to it His Real Presence, with which it had never been endowed before.

drink-offering;" circumcision was changed to baptism; but God's Elect were still the members of His Church, good, bad, and indifferent. We claim that, as in Jewish times, so now, God calls upon His Elect, each and all, to make their Election sure by using their privileges and divinely-given helps in the Church aright; we claim that as the Jews, good, bad, and indifferent, were addressed as the Elect, so likewise the Apostles addressed *all* the members of the Ephesian, the Corinthian, the Roman, the Philippian and the Colossian Church, good, bad, and indifferent, as the Elect; and furthermore, that the Bible warns us, that every individual branch in Christ that beareth not fruit, although in Christ, although baptized into His Body, although of the Elect, will be cut off eventually and not attain to salvation. We claim, therefore, that the Church, the great Catholic Body Mystical, the divinely-given means of assistance, is a most important factor, bearing upon the salvation of souls; important because to be grafted into it by baptism is to be grafted into Christ; important, from the aids it renders the sinner by its Rites, Ordinances, Ministry, and Sacraments, as he toils along his hard way toward salvation. With us, therefore, Election is generic;* the Election is the body of the Church

* "Furthermore," says the XVIIth Article, "we must receive God's promises in such wise as they be *generally* set forth to us in Holy Scripture." *Generally*, i. e. not, "For the most part," but, as opposed to *particularly* or *individually;* not *usually*, but *uni-*

Catholic. With the Protestant sects, Election is individual.

You sometimes hear the phrase, "No church without a Bishop." I do not mean to deny this. But I would direct your attention away from this as a superficial point, and beneath it to this question of Election, as after all the *Articulus Ecclesiæ stantis vel cadentis.*

Now, whichever side is right—and I do not propose to discuss this point—you cannot fail to perceive at once that here is a very radical difference between the two; a difference in accordance with which a hundred and one subsequent questions are decided—the question of the ministry, the question of the sacraments, the entire question of the Church Visible. For, if Election be of separate individuals to life eternal, irrespective of any ecclesiastical means, what do you want of a great Visible Church Catholic on earth, with its regular Apostolic Ministry, with its Rites, with its identical Life running all the way through time, God-given and Divine? That Church disappears at once from your necessities. She is no longer needed with Her baptism as a medium of union between the Sinner and Christ, and Her Eucharist as a life-nourisher. But, on the contrary, the idea of a Church invisible, consisting of all holy persons in all denominations, and even

versally, or better, *generically;* that is to say, as concerning *classes of persons.* The word employed in the Latin form of the Article is *generaliter*, not *plerumque.*

out of them, takes Her place. I say "out of them;" for Holy Baptism is either what I have designated it, an amazing reality, or else it is nothing. Under the Protestant idea of Election it becomes immaterial to the individual, except from policy or taste's sake, what form of Church organization he adopts. For, at any rate, he is elected, aside from any earthly appliances, directly to salvation. If the Methodists deny this, then with them Election amounts to nothing at all; there is no such thing as Election. But alas for this; the whole Bible, Old and New Testament, is full of an Election, a *selection* of some kind. While to us the whole earthly appliance of the Church is no mere matter of taste, but is divinely given as the best possible means for man's assistance and is therefore sacred; to the Protestant a visible form of the Church becomes a matter of mere human propriety. In his intense individualism, all organizations as Protestant corporate bodies are logically unnecessary. It becomes immaterial whether he has the Apostolic line of ministerial succession or not. All that is really wanted is for some one, whether ordained at all or not makes no difference, to tell the sinner "to come to Christ" in some indefinite way. If he is elect, he will be saved; if he is not elect, all the Church Catholics, and all the divinely-given Ministries and Sacraments in the world will not mend the matter a whit for him. Thus the whole Protestant system of individualism, with its destruction of the Church and Her Ministry and Rites and Ways, takes the place of the great Catholic idea of the organic Church, as a part of God's plan wrought out in Christ to help the sinner in making his calling and election sure. With us the Church comes in as a medium of union with Christ; with the Protestant as an interference.

For fifteen hundred years after Christ there had been four factors in the scheme of salvation, viz.: God, the God-man Christ, His Body Mystical or Church, and the sinner. The sinner was, by baptism, grafted into the Body Mystical or Church, and thus made one with Christ; and by the Holy Eucharist fed with Him; and being one with the Son, was made one with the Father also. For first, Father and Son are one; second, God and Man are one in Christ; third, Christ and His Church are one; and lastly, the Sinner becomes one with the whole by the uniting element of baptism. But at the Reformation, Protestantism, consistent with its idea of individual Election to eternal life, struck out the Church; and this was exactly what our Church *did not do*. With that third factor gone, there was at once a gap between the sinner and Christ. How, now, was the sinner to be made one with Christ? Why, Protestantism substituted the process of individual experiencing of religion with the whole revival system; and so sought to bridge the gap between each separate individual and

Christ. And when, without the actual sacramental bands, he falls away, they are forced to bring to bear the machinery again for "a revival of religion in his heart."

Now, the question is not before us, whether the sinner can gain, by that process, the real, the actual, though supernatural, union with Christ, whereby "the twain become one flesh;" or whether it is only that abstract union of consent, which exists between friend and friend. Better the latter, than nothing at all. But there is another very important point which is before us, and that is the logical effect of this system upon sacraments. For, if the individual can either make himself, or become one with Christ under that process, you will see that the importance of baptism at once sinks away; because the main work of uniting the sinner to Christ has all been done without it, and prior to it; and baptism, as a subsequent rite, sinks to a mere form, simply to mark distinction between one set of men and another; a form, which the highly logical society of Quakers get along very well without. Again, if the individual can bridge the gap and become one with Christ, regardless of the Body Mystical, what does he want of the Holy Communion as a visible means to supply him with the strengthening sustenance of Christ's nature? He can feed directly upon Christ, all in the way of *immediation*, all in the way of nature, not of mediation; all in the way of Rationalism, not of Christianity.

For I do not desire, in these solemn and vital questions, to disguise what I mean. Strike out the Sacraments, strike out the Church Catholic as Christ's Body Mystical, as the Outward Means of conveying Inward Graces; strike out the Apostolic Ministry, and you have struck a fatal blow at the whole doctrine of Mediation between man and God. You have sounded the trumpet for Immediation. You do not, as some excellent people fancy, start an issue between Catholic Christianity and a merely spiritual kind of Christianity. Your issue is nothing short of the life or eventual death of Christianity itself. What does the man want, I repeat, of the Holy Eucharist, except as a mere memorial to quicken a memory of a past tragedy on Calvary? A result which preaching, or even his own meditations before a picture, or better, a crucifix, could do as well.

The fact is, with the striking out of the Church, you have even such relics of what is Churchly as are retained by Protestantism, to wit, its sacraments, reduced to mere ordinances—to forms of not very much importance after all, and you have any specified line of ministry to administer those sacraments, a mere impertinence between the sinner and God. Away with your Apostolic Ministry then! says Protestantism; it is no more valid than any other! And Protestantism is entirely logical, too, when it says so. Away with your altars, says the great preacher of Brooklyn; the private Christian layman can set up bread and wine before him in his closet, and gazing upon it can make as valid a Eucharist! and the great preacher is logical and loyal to the principles of Protestantism when he says so. Away with ministerial baptism, say the Se-Baptists; let the layman apply the water to himself, and it is as valid a baptism!

But, did Christ solemnly ordain rites of comparative unimportance, and found a ministry, promising to be with it to the end of the world, the breaking up or continuance of which was a matter of small moment? If not, then there must be something wrong in the point that lies behind and below, that involves all such subsequent destruction. Once restore, however, the lost factor of the Church Catholic, as God's appointed Outward Means of inward graces, and sacraments and ministry all naturally take their places as valuable, nay, as indispensable gifts to mankind.

Now, simply in itself considered, what indeed is the difference whether we have a ministry in three orders or in one? It would seem to be a very small affair either way. And the Church, which stands stiffly for Her Bishops, and refuses to recognize other lines of ministry, would appear to be making a vast deal out of a very unessential matter. But when we consider that there is something beneath this question of the Ministry, which is really, in itself, of vast importance, and that out of it the question of the Apostolic Ministry grows, then the fact, whether or not we are to preserve that ministry, mounts logically into vast importance. Election, and whether it is of the individual to eternal life, or whether it is of the individual into a great system arranged by God Himself, to be, on the whole, the best possible aid to free mortals in struggling toward salvation, is a matter of the utmost importance to dying souls. It is nothing short of two different modes of salvation through Christ, which are presented to the world; the one the individual mode, leaping over the Church, the other the churchly mode; two different modes, each logically destructive of the other. It is nothing short of two different Christs, one with a Body Mystical on earth, the other without it; and finally, two different Gods that are presented to the world. For in its last result the Protestant God is essentially the God of the Sabellian Heresy.

Thus the Apostolic Ministry, as a vital part of that system arranged by God, to be the best help for the sinner in striving to make his calling and election sure, is grounded and rooted in the doctrine of Election. You cannot pull up a tree without tearing up the earth all around it. The ministry, considered merely in itself, may be nothing; the sacraments, and whether they are administered by a divinely authorized set of men or not, may be nothing in themselves; but in their vital connection with Election, with that subject which gives a differing aspect to the whole Christianity which is preached, the Ministry and Sacraments mount,

I repeat, into questions of the gravest importance. It is not strange, it is entirely logical and consistent, that the Protestant sects, with their view of individual Election, should set lightly by any given line of ministry, and be perfectly willing to interchange pulpits indiscriminately. But those among us who tamper with the Ministry and Sacraments of the Church, who set lightly by them, are tampering with, nay, they are upheaving and tearing to pieces the whole ground, and altering the entire aspect of Christianity as presented to the sinner and to the world, by the Church.

You will perceive, then, my friends, that whichever view is right, the Protestant view of Election is, at any rate, absolutely destructive of the whole Church system to which we hold; that as we hold to the other view, it naturally carries us into different conclusions from the Protestant, touching the Ministry, the Sacraments, all the rites and ways, nay the very existence itself of the Church Visible; and that, while all the sects, however differing among themselves on unessential points, are fundamentally at one among themselves, we are separated from them all at the very start by a gulf, not only enormously wide, but enormously deep, and logically incapable of being bridged.

However we may agree with the sects in protesting against certain errors peculiar to Rome, we hold that, at any rate, that fact is not the test by which we should be classified. For we still maintain, that notwithstanding the unfortunate name of "Protestant Episcopal," fixed upon us as an incubus by the notion of a dozen or two gentlemen (to whom, indeed, we are indebted, under God, for very much, for which we are thankful), about the beginning of this century, when the Church in America was marvellously small, we still maintain, I say, that notwithstanding this, we are not one of the sects, that we never have left the great body of the Catholic Church, and that, God helping us, we never will. But that ever, as in the past so in the future, the voice of the Churchman shall be raised in the Creed, "I BELIEVE ONE CATHOLIC AND APOSTOLIC CHURCH."

Even at the risk of exhausting your patience, I ask a few more moments of your attention for a word of warning and of counsel.

It takes no prophetic eye to see that the long night which closed upon the world at the sixteenth century, the long night of mere religious negation, is about over, and that the dawn of religious affirmation, of positive assertion, is breaking again upon the world. Earnest men, tired of being longer told what they shall protest against, what they shall *not* believe, are rising by thousands with the demand upon their lips, "Tell me what I *shall* believe!" We have reached the opening of a tremendous religious crisis in America. A new type of man is coming up with demands other than those born of the mountains of

Switzerland and Scotland. We are beginning to feel all round beneath us, as a people, the ripplings of a mighty tidal wave, which, lifting us, is about to tear our anchors up from the ground of Protestantism, and, if we are not careful, to sweep us *en masse* into Romanism. The reaction has already begun in Boston. How kindly they are beginning to look upon Rome at the spot where all great movements of American mind begin! If you would know which way the storm is going to blow, look at the straws in Boston. The fact is, the position of Protestantism is thoroughly undermined all round about us, and the wary old man of the Vatican knows it. Those two articles in the *Atlantic Monthly* breathe unconsciously the spirit of prophecy. How has all this come to pass? Thus: for nearly a century, now, the cry that has been going up from the laity of all denominations to the pulpit is, "Give us no doctrinal sermons; we simply want practical sermons, sermons that will touch the heart." And what has been the result? Why, throughout this broad land the people everywhere are left to-day without a positive faith of any kind. Seventy years ago, men still believed something; you would not have found, then, an orthodox Congregationalist exchanging pulpits with a Unitarian, nor a Presbyterian with a Methodist. Fifty years ago you would not have found a Baptist coquetting with a Unitarian. Nay, twenty years ago the high Unitarian even shut his pulpit-door against the Parkerite. But *tempora mutantur.*

For the want of positive doctrinal teaching (and Protestantism is in its essence destructive of it, it has all come naturally to pass), positive Christian faith is banished from the land. The faith of America to-day is summed up in this one article, "I believe it is not necessary to believe any thing definite." Now, you may hold the mind of man in the mass at that point for a while, but not long. It is, after all, the nature of the human mind to crave something positive. It will at last react, with a violence of oscillation proportioned to the distance and height to which you have drawn it away.

How stands, then, our beloved country to-day? Why, thus: first, without any definite faith, and unequipped with an argument why it should not believe this theological point, and why it should believe that; and, secondly, with simply a violent prejudice against any thing that is Romish. Now, when Rome makes a convert, she teaches that convert what to believe and why to believe it. And when against American Protestantism, thus emptied of positive faith, unsupplied with theological arguments, and shielded only with brittle prejudices, you bring to bear the positive faith and arguments of Rome, it is like smiting a hollow globe of glass with a boulder of rock. It is the easiest of all things to break down mere uninformed prejudice.

Now, this land, I take it, does not want Romish errors; but it is rising hungry for a positive faith. Christian union meetings, to make headway against Rome, are not the cure of the great disease of the day. That disease can only be met by a positive faith.

Our Church, as a national branch of the great Church Catholic, is not founded upon negations. She is founded upon affirmations. She, as well as Rome, has a positive faith, and not only positive, but clear of any Romish errors. And, unless we rouse to the danger of the day, and with our positive faith go forth to take this land, nothing will save it from Roman Catholicism. Said that remarkable seer, De Tocqueville, years ago, of us, "America will, sooner or later, lie prostrate, the easy captive of Rome; because regulars always beat the militia."

Our duty as loyal children of the Church is plain. We have no need, as we move among the denominations, to apologize for our Fair Mother. Too much of this, alas, already! Too much of the obsequious to our inferiors! "He who excuses, accuses," and but confirms disesteem, instead of commanding respect. We are not *almost* like the denominations, and, therefore, to be tolerated by them in our peculiarities of written prayers and vested clergy. We are Catholic, and fundamentally different. As you go forth, then, into the world as sons and daughters of the Church, sound no uncertain trumpet, but let your motto be, I BELIEVE IN ONE, HOLY, CATHOLIC AND APOSTOLIC CHURCH.

IV.

PROTESTANTISM LOGICALLY DESTRUCTIVE OF CHRISTIANITY.

And many false Prophets shall rise, and shall deceive many.—St. Matt. xxiv. 11.

The New Testament is full of warnings against subtle attacks that were to be made in subsequent times upon Christianity. We are not only told that some of these attacks would be made by open enemies, but that there would be others made by avowed friends. And we are forewarned that the latter would be of such nature as to deceive even the elect were it possible. It is our distinct charge that Protestantism is one of the latter class of attacks. Its adherents are, of course, friends of Christ; but they are mistaken friends; they know not what they do. It is our warning that the sons and daughters of the Church avoid all Protestant religious systems.

We bring forward an additional charge to-day, viz., that wherever you meet with a region of country that has been burned over and over again with the fires of "Revivalism," there an almost utter and very general indifference to religion eventually supervenes. We look not so much at the immediate results of the revival system in making this additional charge; they are deceptive. But we look to the final fruits. The whole system is a stupendous blunder. But even the immediate results are not to be passed over lightly.

Take the great revival of 1859–'60 in Ireland. What is the testimony of the Rev. Isaac Nelson, a Presbyterian minister in Belfast? He frankly says, "The revival was made to rest for its reality on certain extraordinary conversions, which have since proved false and wicked; *the consequence being an immensely increased immorality in Ulster.* Now," he says, "will Dr. McCorle meet us on this assertion, or put it to the test of statistics? We know he will not; he dare not. *The morality of the Presbyterian people has been ruined by the Revival.*" Such, my brethren, was the immediate result, one of the Revivalists himself being the judge.

Let me give you another extract concerning that same Revival; it is this, viz., "Many of the earlier Revivalists, whose mental calibre could not withstand the excitement of the movement, have found a permanent home in lunatic asylums; while multitudes of others, puffed up with spiritual pride, have fallen into worse diseases than that of the mind. Many who, three years ago, were distinguished as Revivalist preachers of the purest and most sanctified kind, are now drunkards, thieves, and immoral livers; and one to our certain knowledge is now lying in prison, charged with being concerned in a late cowardly and barbarous murder. Since the Revival began seduction has prevailed to an extent never known before, as the large increase in the number of illegitimate children fully proves. Has drunkenness or immorality decreased in the district where it chiefly prevailed? The very contrary is the fact. Judged therefore by its results, the Revival movement of 1859–'60 must be considered not as 'a refreshing stream of God's grace,' as some have not hesitated profanely to call it, but as a withering blight which has parched the ground which it seemed to refresh, and has left behind it fruits the full bitterness of which will never be truly known till the day of doom."

But I do not intend in this sermon to dwell at all upon this point of the searing effect of Protestant Revivals. I merely allude to it, and return to one of the main charges, viz.: that wherever the fundamental principles of Protestantism have taken deep root in the mind of a thoughtful people, there, after a number of generations, infidelity prevails to a very general—to an alarming extent. The charge is, that the logical conclusion of the fundamental principles of Protestantism is Rationalism, and that the historical issue in the case of Germany, Switzerland, America, and other Protestant lands, substantiates the logical anticipation.

You perceive at once the seriousness of this

indictment. If it is true, then Protestantism is what I have charged it to be, a heresy. If it is true, it is not a subject to be provoked about; it is a matter to be grieved over; for multitudes of good men are identified with Protestantism. If it is true, Protestantism should be avoided by every one who loves his brother-man, and the cause of our Blessed Saviour. Its houses of worship should never be entered by the sons and daughters of the Church. If it is not true, then it is for Protestants to let us know why, which they have essayed but failed to do hitherto. If it is true, it is something you ought to know and not to turn aside from. If it is true, it is criminal for the Christian to ignore it. It is too important a charge to be prejudged, and too important to be pushed aside because it is an unpleasant subject. If individuals will not hear, the world is hearing, and will hear, and will decide the issue.

There are two counts, then, in the indictment, which I dwell on this morning: First, that, as a fact, infidelity prevails very widely in lands which once were Protestant. Secondly, that this is because the logical issue of the Protestant dogma is Rationalism.

Let us consider the first count. Permit me to read to you a little "Account of Religion in Geneva, Switzerland." It is written by a Protestant minister, and is as follows, viz.:

"The statements made by Mr. J. Wright, a Unitarian, are, alas, too true!—viz., that the successors of the very magistrates who condemned Servetus, of the pastors who excommunicated him as the denier of the Trinity, now themselves unite in *rejecting* that doctrine! The faith of the great churches of Geneva is Unitarianism. The system of John Calvin is almost extinct in the town where he was once the spiritual tyrant. There are believers in the divinity of our blessed Lord Jesus existing in Geneva, it is true, who are divided into several parties, but the national church of Geneva is Unitarian. The number of inhabitants in Geneva amounts to about 64,000; *among them are about* 40,000 *Unitarians*, 18,000 *Roman Catholics, and the miserable balance only are left to Protestant Trinitarianism.*"

We all know how things have turned out after three centuries of Protestantism in Germany. There is no need of testimony on that point.

We all know how it is in New England, and wherever New England emigration has spread. But let me read you an extract in illustration. Not many months since, the *Hartford Courant* informed us that "the Congregational ministers of Connecticut have thoroughly canvassed their parishes to ascertain the actual religious condition of the State. The result was unexpected. In one hundred towns, at least one-third of the families are not in the habit of going to church. Irreligion was found to increase in proportion to the distance from the centre of the towns. It prevails more in sparsely-settled farming districts than in the manufacturing villages. The Committee on Home Evangelization say in their published report:

"'The returns give the impression that the Roman Catholic population do not often sink to so low a grade of heathenism as the irreligious native-born population. They do not entirely abandon some thought of God, and some respect for their own religious observances. *Uniformly the districts most utterly given over to desolation* are districts occupied by a population purely native American. A similar state of things is reported to exist in some parts of Massachusetts.'"

Now, brethren, I am not, of course, defending Roman Catholicism. But it is at least singular to notice that of the two evils in Connecticut, Romanism and Protestantism, that which with all its errors is still Catholic, is, according to the official testimony of Protestants themselves, the lesser evil.

Now, let us see what is going on among the Presbyterians. Some years ago there was a long article in the *New York Observer* (Old School) in eulogy of an excellent "Elect Lady," who was especially commended for knowing the Westminster Catechism by heart, and teaching it carefully to her descendants. The *Observer* then went on to say: "There are few among us now, fewer in proportion than in previous years, of whom such a fact can be affirmed! What is the reason? Is the catechism obsolete? Is it a bad instruction for our children?" Now, brethren, this is a very important confession, showing the downward tendency of Protestantism in the Presbyterian ranks. Nor is this confined to Presbyterianism in the United States. At the antipodes it is as bad or worse. Permit me to read to you the following item from a dissenting paper in England:

"From some proceedings before the Presbytery of Tasmania on the 22d of April, it appears that one of their number, the Rev. Mr. Robertson, is charged with entertaining unsound views on Baptism and the Lord's Supper, having *a tendency to Unitarianism. The Presbytery declined by a majority* to file a libel on Mr. Robertson. The Rev. Mr. J. Storie then said that he and those who thought with him had determined, in case a majority of the Presbytery acquitted Mr. Robertson, to apply to the Home Government to withhold the grant from the Church of Scotland in this colony, on the ground that *the majority of the Presbytery had apostatized from the faith of their fathers.* The Rev. Dr. Turnbull and the Rev. J. Walker concurred in the statement of Mr. Storie; and Mr. Walker remarked that the Presbytery must *either be purified or swept away altogether.*"

Look at Harvard University, once Trinitarian, but descending, after a while, into Unitarianism. Yale College was established, if I mistake not, owing to the Unitarianism of Harvard. But, at any rate, years ago, President Clap, on entering upon his duties at Yale, "publicly acknowledged not only the Westminster Catechism and Confession of Faith and the Saybrook Platform, but also the Apostles', Nicene, and Athanasian Creeds as agreeing with the word of God." The gradual but steady degeneracy of the Protestant system *would*, however, work out its own results. And so we find that President Stiles differed from his predecessor. Dr. Stiles would not accept the office of President until the corporation had abrogated the tests instituted by President Clap, with the exception of the Saybrook Platform. The Saybrook Platform held its own till 1822, when all tests were abrogated. "Thus in regard to the formal teaching of theology in the 'Church of Christ in Yale College,' as required by statute, it began with full, definite, established formulas of Faith, and ended in—nothing." But the evidences of the inevitable descent of Protestantism from the high standards of faith and practice, which it carried with it out of the Church, are varied as well as numerous. Time was, for instance, when the vast majority of Protestants held it to be right to baptize their infants. The decay of infant baptism among them is another token that they are sinking from the faith of their fathers. The annual report (1860) of the Congregational General Association of Connecticut informs us that there were "many instances of Congregational societies, numbering their members by hundreds, but having not one infant baptism through the year." But I might fill this sermon with similar extracts.

I pass on to lay before you reasons, additional to those presented in previous sermons, why the logical result of Protestantism is Rationalism.

It is patent that, in Massachusetts and else where, whole orthodox Congregational Societies have gone down as bodies into Unitarianism. Now, if individuals only had gone, they might be considered as eccentric cases. But where societies have gone as bodies, pastor and the majority of his people, it shows that there was some logical necessity about it.

If, too, this descent of Presbyterianism into Congregationalism, and of Trinitarian Congregationalism into old-fashioned Unitarianism, and of old high Unitarianism into Parkerism, was only to be found in isolated cases, or in one section of a country, or even in one country, or in one century only, we might think it had happened from individual peculiarity, or from local causes, or from national idiosyncrasy. But when the evidences of the grand descent are everywhere where Protestantism has been, and not even confined to one century, there must be some logical necessity about it to account for it. Why, look at England in 1656. Protestantism was at first Presbyterian there. But the English mind was a logical mind, and Presbyterianism was not long in giving birth to Congregationalism (or Independentism), which grew in Cromwell's day into far larger proportions than those of the mother that bore it.

Everywhere we find every thing indicating the downward movement.

I proceed, then, to give a reason, additional to those set forth in previous sermons, for this gravity.

The great truths which distinguish Christianity are the Mediation, the Priesthood, the Royalty, and the Sacrifice of Christ. These truths have their natural, visible expressions in the Church Apostolic and Catholic. What are those expressions? First, how does the spiritual fact of Christ's Mediation find its corresponding expression in the Church? Why, in all those peculiarities which come in between the sinner and God, and which are intermediate, not for the purpose of sundering but of uniting the two. There are, for instance, the sacraments and ordinances of the Church; the separation of the holy altar from the nave by a railing; the fact that the layman approaches to the rail and no farther; and, in fact, all the intermediate rites and ceremonies of the Church. Secondly, how does the spiritual fact of Christ's Priesthood find its visible expression in the Church? Why, in the apostolic clergy on earth, who act for the laity; who alone can consecrate and administer the Blessed Eucharist. Thirdly, where, in the Church, do we find the visible expression of Christ's Royalty, His authority as King? We find it in the government that God hath set over His Church Militant; in the Rector as the governor of the Parish, and the

Bishop as the governor of the Rectors and laity. Then, fourthly, the Sacrifice of Christ finds its visible expression in the Blessed Eucharist.

Now, in every family the children are in a natural school; as from earliest infancy they look up to their earthly father, they are gaining impressions touching what God must be as their Heavenly Father; they are learning to look up to, reverence, and obey Him. Just so God would set us all in the school of the Church; that, trained in that school, and under the constant influence of the four visible expressions I have mentioned, we may not lose our hold of the prime facts of the Mediation, the Priesthood, the Royalty, and the Sacrifice of Christ.

Now, Protestantism has striven to turn the world out of that school; and what wonder if, in the end, its adherents lose knowledge of, and belief in, those prime facts!

For let us try the effect of the destruction of any one of the four visible expressions. The cry of the Protestant is, "I want no visible Church; I want nothing of the kind to come in between me and God; I want no rails at chancels; I want no communion-table shut up in an apartment by itself; bring it down into the congregation; your whole visible scheme of intermediation is in the way; it is impertinent; I can and will go direct to God myself without your cumbersome churchly machinery; I want no set lessons from Scripture selected for my contemplation on set days;

I can select for myself; I want no days set apart by the Church in which I must meditate on certain truths; I can think of any of those truths at any time." And so Protestantism, borne on by its spirit of liberty, so called, clears away the whole.

You can go direct to God, indeed, Mr. Protestant? Our scheme of visible intermediation in the way and impertinent? Ah, brethren, do you not see that this strikes at the *principle of any mediation whatever?* By such assertions Protestantism yields the vital principle itself to Rationalism. And it is not at all strange that, in the hands of such giants as Beecher, Channing, and Parker, the Protestant mind should slowly sink into avowed Rationalism. Here is the explanation of the fact, that thousands of young and middle-aged men, sons and grandsons of the old-fashioned Protestants, are either secret doubters or avowed skeptics; and that our very churches are crowded with semi-Deists, who chafe under any preaching save the preaching of glittering generalities about morality and natural goodness. The fact is, in abandoning God's Visible Church Catholic, Protestants have abandoned the vital outwork of the doctrine of Mediation—the sole defence of that doctrine; and with the outwork gone, the city itself falls. It is fatal to touch that in the Church Visible which is harmonious with, and which expresses and conserves the great truth of, the Mediation.

Try now the effect of the destruction of the

outwork or bulwark of the Priesthood of Christ, the second great spiritual fact of Christianity. Strike down the Apostolic ministry of the Visible Church Catholic, and you equally expose the spiritual fact of the Priesthood of Christ. And thus laid bare and unprotected, it also falls before the attacks of Rationalism. Let us look at this a little:

The Protestant cry is, "There is no such thing as a visible Priesthood on earth; the ministry need not originate from the apostles alone, and come down in the regular succession which the Catholics claim; it originates as well from the people, in whom primarily its powers are lodged." In other words, as a recent writer says, "The people and not the apostles are the true ultimate source of ecclesiastical and ministerial power;" the Christian ministry, according to the Protestant cry, "are not a distinct order of men; and hence there is no such thing as a Christian Priesthood in distinction from the people at large." "Every man his own priest to God," is the popular cry.

Every man his own priest to God, indeed, Mr. Protestant? *Nothing* between God and man? Ah, beloved, do you not perceive that Protestantism, though it may not yield all at once the naked fact of the spiritual priesthood of Christ, has, after all, by this fatal step, yielded the principle of any priesthood whatever? Do you not see that, with the vital principle gone, with the *practical* denial of the principle rooted in their minds, the mere intellectual notion of Christ's Priesthood, which they still retain for a while, has been undermined, and will sooner or later fall, if not in the first generation, then in the second, third, or fourth? It must logically fall, and, alas, it does fall practically! It will not do to tamper with that fundamental feature of God's Church, namely, the Apostolic ministry. It will not do to raise to a level with it a ministry whose ultimate source of authority is laymen or unauthorized presbyters, instead of the Holy Apostles; for, as the fountain cannot rise higher than its spring, the rearing of such a man-made ministry is the breaking down of all ministry to a level with laymen; and this is simply and solely and logically a blow at the cherished Priesthood of Christ Itself.

A similar course of remark might be made on the government of the Church, which is the visible expression on earth of the spiritual truth of the Royalty of Christ, and which is the school in which God in His wisdom has set us, that we may learn and not lose the knowledge of that prime fact. And a similar course of remark might be made on the Blessed Eucharist as the conserver of the fact of the Sacrifice of Christ. But enough has been said to show how Protestantism is logically destructive of Christianity.

Think of the millions it has drawn away from Christ; think how it has sapped the foundations of Christianity! My friends, these are words not calculated to be popular; but they are words that need to be spoken. When some poor bewildered mind goes over to Rome, some Churchmen roll up eyes of holy horror; but they forget the vastly more serious events that are taking place in the opposite direction. We are not so much in danger of superstition as we are of skepticism. I would have you mark *this*, my beloved, I would have you meditate upon it, I would have you repeat it to your friends, viz., that those exceptional cases that have gone to Rome are as a single star to all the myriads of stars in comparison with the thousands who have fallen innocently and unconsciously into the fatal drift of Protestantism, and been sucked down at last into the rushing swirl of Unitarianism and the dreadful vortex of Infidelity.

As I make this assertion, you will not understand me as saying that it is the first generation which passes out of the Church into Protestantism that runs this entire career into Rationalism. It is only here and there that you find a person with brain enough to pass the entire distance from the top to the bottom of the logical slope. I could point you to one, whom we all know by reputation, that started as a high Presbyterian, and has now reached the point of low Congregationalism, which is but a shade above high Unitarianism. And then I could point you to another, now dead, whose fame was world-wide, that started as a young man at the point of high Unitarianism, and ran the rest of the logical career into Rationalism. Such, I say, are rare cases. Nay, it is, in general, only successive generations that run the full career. The mass of mind moves slowly down a logical slope. But man is logical, and the mass of mind moves surely and inevitably. The Methodists, as a body, have already in one hundred years moved too far down the slope, and gathered too much momentum, ever to come back to the Catholic summit of the hill. Individuals may get back, but, as a body, Methodism is doomed.

When, beloved, a mother, leaving our Church, goes to Presbyterianism, she thinks she is merely exchanging one form of Christianity for another; that it is, to all intents and purposes, a venial, a harmless change. She has no idea that she has leaped the immense gulf that lies between Christianity and incipient Rationalism. But when she has taken the step, what has she done? She has done all she can to give her children a heritage of Congregationalism, her grandchildren a heritage of Unitarianism, and her great-grandchildren a heritage of Infidelity.

There are great warnings against Rome. Well, Rome is an evil. But it is time the solemn word was spoken, and spoken boldly, of warning against the far worse evil of Protestantism. It is time men understood that Protestantism is an awful and most dangerous heresy.

V.

PROTESTANTISM THE SECOND GREAT HERESY OF THE CHRISTIAN ERA.

"But there were false prophets also among the people, even as there shall be false teachers among you, who privily shall bring in damnable heresies, even denying the Lord that bought them, and bring upon themselves swift destruction. And many shall follow their pernicious ways; by reason of whom the way of truth shall be evil spoken of."—2 PETER ii. 1, 2.

IN fulfilment of this prophecy, many heresies have arisen and swarmed around Christianity. Each has had its venomous sting. But there are three monstrous forms of the brood, before which all the others are quite insignificant. The first of these was Arianism; the second was Protestantism; and the third is modern "Criticism," represented by Strauss, Rénan, Colenso, and others. All other forms of heresy struck at the superstructure and pinnacles of Christianity, but these three enormous heresies have their bad preëminence because they struck or strike at Her very foundations. For if, as I showed in the second discourse, the Bible rests on the Church, it is no less true that Christianity rests on the double support of the Church and the Bible. Touch either of the two, and Her position becomes more than critical, for She must fall. Permit me to change the figure. Christianity stands secure behind two allied armies, viz., the Church and the Bible. As long as these armies mutually support each other, and neither of them is broken, Christianity is safe.

Now, so far as human ingenuity can conceive at present, there are only three ways by which Christianity can be exposed from behind Her protection, rendered helpless, and slain: First, the Church may be directly attacked; second, the two allied bodies, viz., the Church and the Bible, may be set in antagonism with each other; or third, the Bible may be directly attacked.

Take the first case. The Church, as a visible organic body, as the Body Mystical of Christ, depends for Her very life upon Christ. Destroy the God-man within Her, and you have struck down Her life; you have reduced Her to a dead body, and Christianity will fall. This attack was made by the heresiarch Arius. This attack was the boldest of the three against Christianity. Suffice it to say, though Christianity was, humanly speaking, in critical position for years, the attack failed. Arius did not intend to take the life of Christianity; but he was none the less an heresiarch for all his good intentions.

Now take the second case. As Christianity stood secure behind her two mutually supporting armies, viz., the Church and the Bible, instead of a direct attack on either army, the two armies could be set fighting each other; and so Christianity become exposed. This was done by Protestantism. This was the meanest mode of attack. I do not say that Calvin and Luther and Zwinglius and the rest of them intended to destroy Christianity any more than Arius did. Very far from it. But they were none the less heresiarchs for that. For, brethren, we are looking at the whole movement from a stand-point where we can take in both worlds at once—this world and the world beneath. And we must judge such movements by their logical and historical results, and not merely by the good motives of the men who were engaged in them. It was none the less disastrous to the patient whose eye was put out, that the bungling oculist only sought to remove an irritating particle. We must consider the disastrous effects of the Continental Reformation on the souls of men to-day, if we would get at the other cause that was operating in it besides the men who trod the earth. Protestantism made an ally of the Bible, and with it flew at the Church to destroy Her. I do not deny that the Church needed reforming. But a call for reformation is very different from a call for destruction. Satan, however, saw his advantage, and picked his men. I do not acquit the obstinacy of the Ultra-montanism of the day. It was maddening to the other party; and doubtless Satan had something to do with it. But it was in order that he might use it to fire up Protestantism as his main engine of evil. Suffice it to say, Protestantism, making an ally of the Bible, succeeded, not in reforming the Church, but in attacking and destroying Her in many lands. And so we have the sad spectacle of a prostrate Christianity in those lands.

The *Evening Post*, in its last evening's issue, in speaking of the "Aspects of Religious Life in Germany," says: "A letter on this subject appears in the *Methodist*, written by Rev. Abel Stevens, a leading scholar of his denomination, who has taken great pains to become familiarly acquainted with the domestic and inner life of the people of Germany. He confesses that, after five visits, and much careful observation, living in many families, and travelling on foot among the villages, he does not yet fairly understand their religious condition." But, brethren, the rest of the world are beginning to understand it, and to brand its cause with the mark it deserves. I continue the quotation: "Their country," says this reverend gentleman, "is studded with antique churches; their history is full of religious achievements; their traditions full of religious legends; their universities rife with religious polemics; but there is apparently no religious life in the heart of the race, if you except the peculiar little parties of pietists, Moravians, and Methodists, who really are exceptional to the whole modern genius of the people. Indifference to all vital religion seems to be a characteristic of the mass of the Germanic race. They appear to have exhausted their old interest in it, after so many struggles and revolutions of opinion and criticism, and now turn away from it as if tired of it, and waiting for something new as a substitute." He thinks that "religious indifference is the leading characteristic of the masses, as free-thinking and materialism are of the cultivated classes, and that between them religious life has mostly died out. Few of the men ever go to church, and few religious forms remain in families, while Sunday has become a holiday, on which the bier-garten is the chief place of resort."

Brethren, add Switzerland to Germany, and call to mind, as a type-fact of the state of things there, that Calvin's own parish is in the very dregs of Unitarianism, and that the very pulpit from which that violent man thundered is now occupied by a Rationalist. Add New England, and count the "Orthodox Congregational" Societies that have gone over as bodies to Unitarianism in the past century, and then count the Unitarian parishes that have gone down to Ultra-Parkerism. There are fossil Unitarians in New England; there are reactionary Unitarians; but the real thinkers and the great body of the laymen are going where logic points, and are to-day out-Parkering Parker himself in their denial of Christianity. The latter class command, at least, our respect for their consistency. The reactionary class may inspire us with hope; but the fossils are unworthy of mention.

Now, brethren, if Unitarianism started simply with the view of teaching a better idea of God than had been taught, but without the slightest design of destroying the Bible, and if it has resulted (as indeed it has) in logically producing a Theodore Parker school of thought destructive of the Bible, then it is very evident that Unitarianism, considered *as a preserver of the Bible*, is a failure. So, equally, if Protestantism started with the view of preserving Christianity, but only of teaching a better system of Christianity than that taught by the Church Catholic, and if it ends logically in destroying fundamental Christian truth, and historically in plunging the vast majority of thinking men, in the lands where it has had sway, into skepticism and mere natural religion, then surely Protestantism *as a system for the preservation of Christianity* is a consummate failure, an awful cheat, a delusion for souls. By all sound logic Protestantism ought to go down into Unitarianism, and then Unitarianism die out in Parkerism and bald Rationalism. Now, if this logical anticipation stood alone, unfortified by historical fact, persons might be justified in feeling that, however fair the logic looked, there might be some flaw in it somewhere. If, on the other hand, regardless of any logical anticipation, it had historically happened that peoples, once Protestant, had each somehow or other become Rationalistic, then we might be justified in saying that perhaps it ought not to have been so logically, but that some other cause came in to send them down and out of Christianity. But where logic anticipates the historical issue, and the historical fact confirms the logical anticipation, the case is about closed. If Protestantism has not signally failed in preserving Christianity, then pray where has it succeeded?

Don't point me to advance in science, and education, and invention; all that isn't Protestantism. Electricity, and the needle-gun, and the education of the masses, and such like, are as consistent with the spirit and prevalence of Catholicity as they are with the spirit and prevalence of Protestantism. Nor do I assert that Protestantism was an unmitigated evil. Satan is always ready to give away a sixpence worth of good, if under the cover of such generosity he can gain a dollar's worth of evil. Then, again, do not regard me as condemning persons. There is a difference between condemning persons and condemning their systems. Persons are to be judged by their motives; systems by their results. To stab Christianity to the heart was the very last thing Calvin and Luther intended to do. But that the result of their principles is logically, and has been historically, what I state, is patent. That there will be some—mere creatures of prejudice, and blind as bats; and that there will be others—moved by social and public position, who will not see all this, and who will be either pro voked at the assertion that Protestantism has failed, or will for a time pass the matter over with a supercilious smile, is to be expected. They are to be pitied. They do not know the earthquake forces that are working under them. For I am stating to you, brethren, simply what thousands upon thousands (I do not exaggerate), here and across the water, have been feeling for a long time—namely, that Protestantism is Satan clothed in the garments of light. Brethren, you are going to see Unitarianism grow into a large body; for it is destined to fatten and grow huge for a time on the carcass of dying Trinitarian Protestantism. The mission of Unitarianism as a destroyer is not yet closed on earth.

Thus Arianism attacked one of the foundations of Christianity, viz., the Church. Protestantism set the two foundations, viz., Bible and Church, a-knocking against each other. I repeat, so far as human ingenuity can at present conceive, only one more really great heretical antagonist to Christianity is possible, namely, an antagonist that shall make a direct assault on the Bible. This last assault has now been commenced by the Critical School of France, Germany, and England. If the first was the boldest attack, and the second the meanest, this third and last is the most intellectual and respectable. Arianism is dead (for modern Unitarians are not Arians); Protestantism is dying by inches, and "Criticism" is rising to be our real, robust, and dangerous foe. The rise of the "Critical School" is not strange. Alas, poor Protestantism, that very Private Judgment, which she summoned up to rush at and destroy the Church, now made strong by exercise, and bold by petting and encouragement, turns to tear her Bible with its talons, and prey upon her own bosom. The very rise of these two determined and already large schools, viz.: the Catholic and the Infidel Free Thinking, and their common recoil away from Protestantism, the former in the direction of the old defences, where Church and Bible can stand together and impregnable, and the latter in the direction of an earnest, honest, but blind clutching after truth, is an additional evidence of the failure of Protestantism as a system. Permit me here to quote the language of a late English article which I read day before yesterday, and which is in exact accord with what I have said in this course of sermons. "There can be," the writer says, "only Catholic Christianity and Rationalism; only those who fall back on that point of Church authority abandoned at the Reformation, or those who seek out a new basis for the reconstruction of religion. That a few will hold on still to what is demonstrably untenable is only what is to be expected. But it will be only those mentally incapacitated for realizing the weakness of their position, or those who allow their reason to be distorted by their prejudice. The vast majority of intelligent persons are already convinced that Christianity must have some other hold-fast than Scripture alone, if the Faith is not to be swept away into the ocean of unbelief."

One of the most noteworthy signs of the times is a wide-spread yearning for unity. Catholics both in England and America are holding out the olive-branch to the Methodists; and other analogous movements are taking place both in Rome and in the Greek Church. I have already called your attention to the fact that while Protestantism has no common creed, the Catholic Church, however her parts may differ from each other, has, underneath those differences, a common Creed, a common Ministry, and common Sacraments. For our Church does not assert that there are "only two Sacraments;" but that there are two only which are generically necessary to salvation. She gives to the other five the title of "Sacraments" also. Now, here, in this common Ministry, faith and Sacraments, is the sole basis of any unity that is possible in Christendom. It is not necessary that all the parts, Greek, Roman, and Anglican, should shape themselves after one precise pattern. This would be a unity of simplicity, not the larger, more developed unity of multiplexity. This would be the unity of the seed, not the great complex unity of the tree. It is not necessary that there be one ritual for all. Men are of different races. There is the ardent Slavonic, the less warm Latin, and the comparatively cold Anglican. Each has his own tastes and instincts, and religious demands. A ritual which, to us, would be glorious with ceremonial, would chill an Eastern, or Greek, to death with its apparent coldness. He needs more to express the same thing than we do. Why should one race of men impose its ritual on another? Our truths are deeper than our rituals. We want no rigid uniformity either in manner or thought in the Catholic Church. Our faith, Ministry, and Sacraments, are one already. All that we lack is such modification in doctrine, in each of the parts, as will enable a restoration of intercommunion to take place between the three, a mutual recognition again between the brothers of the same one family, and common organic action against the common enemy, the world. We want a recognition of the unity between the parts; not an absorption of either part into another. Excessive legislation on small points, the miserable desire to be perpetually tinkering, and over-sensitiveness on minor differences, have been the vices of the Church Catholic. We forget that there is a great body of general health in Her, which will in time throw off poisonous secretions if the latter are let quietly alone.

But all this brings me to another point. I showed in the second sermon of this course, that while Protestantism gets the Church from the Bible, Catholicity gets the Bible from the Church. But their ideas are radically different as to what the Church is. The Protestant notion is, that "a Church is an aggregation of individuals who hold in common a certain theological system gathered out of the Scripture." Thus the basis of their unity is intellect. With them Sacraments are not, as we are taught by our Prayer Book, instruments by which God doth work invisibly in us; but they are rather "seals and pledges of a grace that has already been given." Protestantism makes "an intellectual process called faith, and a mental conviction called apprehension of Christ by faith, to be the means of effecting a union between the individual and Christ." Therefore it were a mere form to baptize infants. But with Catholicism, on the other hand, the Church is not a mere aggregation of intellectually-consenting individuals, each of whom has passed through this intellectual process and had this mental conviction. But the Church is a Living Body, having a corporate Head; a Visible Body with an Invisible Life. That Life, that Soul of the Church, is Christ. He moves over the earth in His Body mystical, and is as really present, and acting, and speaking, to-day in that Body, as He was eighteen hundred years ago, when He was on earth in His Body natural. We call you to no merely intellectual accord with a Being of long ago. We call you to no mere memory of a Being who passed away eighteen hundred years ago. Catholicity has not dropped Christ into the past, and lost Him as a real existence, retaining simply a memory and an intellectual conception of Him. She still has Him. She gives you the very Being at whose feet St. Mary sat. He is here now in His Body Mystical, still going forth to you, still ready to feed you. With Catholicity the members of the Body Mystical are grafted into Its divine life by the Sacrament of Baptism, which was divinely appointed to that end; and they partake of Its divine life unto their spiritual development, through Its means of grace, and especially Its Blessed Eucharist. Catholicity holds that the union with Christ thus supernaturally effected by God in baptism is "irrespective of any exercise of the intellect, but is a free gift of God," where there is no bar; and that, therefore, infants may and should be baptized. Thus the Catholic is a spiritual not an intellectual system. Its basis of unity is Christ, and not man's intellect. The Catholic, I say, holds that Christ is really within the Church, and that life and truth are to spread from Him through His Body Mystical on earth. Furthermore, the Catholic holds that, "in order to the extension and communication of this spiritual life and grace, our Lord appointed a ministry in His Church, whose office is to administer the means of grace to its members; and that He appointed the Apostles to this office with power to transmit their commission to others in an orderly way, as the needs of the Body required," and so on till the end of time. This is another distinction between Catholicity and Protestantism. I take it I need do no other than simply refer you to your Prayer

Book, and leave you to decide whether our Church is Protestant or Catholic.

In conclusion, "The Church has authority in matters of faith," says the Prayer Book. "Nay," says Protestantism, "the individual judgment hath authority in matters of faith; and, if one of 'our churches' does not harmonize in its faith with my notions, I have a perfect right to shake off the dust from my feet at its doors, and go forth and organize another 'Church.'" And so he has, brethren; so he has; we don't deny that. One human institution is as good as another, and all together, so far as the salvation of souls five hundred years hence is concerned, are not worth the paper their constitutions and long declarations of doctrine are written upon. It doesn't take many centuries for the whole pack of them to tumble over each other down into the valley of oblivion.* So he has, I repeat, a perfect right to

* Below is a list of sects (by no means a complete list) which have buzzed about the Catholic Church. Some of them grew to enormous size in their day, and lasted several centuries; but their names even sound strangely to modern ears. The numbers indicate the centuries in which the sects arose:

1 Docithians.
1 Nicolaitans.
1 Saturninians.
2 Millennarians.
2 Basilides.
2 Epiphanians.
2 Hydroparasites.
2 Melitonians.
2 Saccophori.
2 Severians.
2 Ophites.
2 Alogi.
2 Abelites.
2 Colarbasians.
2 Cerdonians.
2 Ossenians.
2 Marcionites.
2 Proclianites.
2 Serpentinians.
2 Cainites.
2 Valentinians.
2 Cerinthians.
2 Nazareans.
2 Apotactics.

go forth and organize another "Church." And thus we have a "Church" organized by LUTHER, and another "Church" organized by CALVIN, and another "Church" organized by CAMPBELL, and

2 Montanists.
2 Adamites.
2 Materialists.
2 Archontics.
2 Ebionites.
2 Marcites.
2 Antitactæ.
2 Elxaites.
2 Alogians.
2 Hermogenians.
2 Ascodrogites.
2 Ascodrutes.
2 Encratites.
2 Carpocratians.
2 Bardesamites.
2 Artemonites.
2 Artotyrites.
2 Marcellans.
2 Ascetics.
2 Sethians.
2 Lucianists.
2 Quintilians.
2 Florinians.
2 Elcesaites.
2 Patripassians.
3 Novatians.
3 Passalorynchites.
3 Eternals.
3 Asclepidoteans.
3 Noetians.
3 Paulianists.
3 Athocians.
3 Apocarites.
3 Beryllians.
3 Manichæans.
3 Hieracites.
3 Adelphians.
3 Aquilinians.
3 Arabians.
3 Valetians.
3 Solitaries.
4 Eusebians.
4 Psathyrians.
4 Heloidans.
4 Vigilantians.
4 Luciferians.
4 Jovinianists.
4 Heracleonites.
4 Macedonians.
4 Incorruptibles.
4 Colluthians.
4 Arians.
4 Pneumato-Machists.
4 Apollinarians.
4 Accacians.
4 Semi-Arians.
4 Meletians.
4 Priscillianists.
4 Tascodrugitæ.
4 Messalians or Enchites.
4 Photinians.
4 Donatists.
4 Anthropomorphites.
4 Docetæ.
4 Psaltyrians.
4 Anomœans.
4 Audæans.
4 Eudoxians.
4 Eunomians.
4 Assuritans.
4 Satamans.
4 Collyridians.
4 Eustathians.
4 Abelonians.
4 Euphratesians.
4 Aerians.
4 Sabellians.
4 Ætians.
5 Nestorians.
5 Cœlicolæ.
5 Angelites.
5 Patricians.
5 Theopaschites.
5 Pelagians.
5 Eutychians.
5 Monophysites.
5 Semi-Pelagians.
5 Mopsuetians.
5 Acephali.
5 Armenians.
5 Predestinarians.
6 Accemetæ.
6 Agnoites.
6 Barsanians.

another "Church" organized by GEORGE FOX, and a great many others, organized by I know not whom. But in the language of a venerable presbyter of Massachusetts, "I have somewhere read that the

6 Tritheites.
6 Corrupticolæ.
6 Gaianitæ.
6 Paulicians.
6 Damianists.
6 Cononites.
7 Chazinzarians.
7 Ethnophrones.
7 Agynians.
7 Maronites.
7 Agonyclitæ.
7 Monothelites.
8 Albanenses.
8 Adoptionists.
9 Abrahamites.
10 Paterines.
11 Berengarians.
12 Pasaginians.
12 Albigenses.
12 Waldenses.
12 Tanguelinians.
12 Gazares.
12 Henricians.
12 Leucopetrians.
12 Bogomiles.
12 Apostles.
12 Circumcelliones.
13 Wilhelminians.
13 Almericians.
13 Flagellants.
13 Carthari.
13 Bethlehemites.
13 Brethren and Sisters of the Free Spirit.
14 Wickliffites.
14 Dulcinists.
14 Barlaamites.
14 Dancers.
14 Albati.
14 Quietists.
15 Adiaphorists.
15 Hussites.
15 Calixtines.
15 Orevites.
15 Orphans.
15 Taberites.
15 Bohemian Brethren.
15 White Brethren.
16 Brownists.
16 Flemingians.
16 Erastians.
16 Budnæans.
16 Davidists.
16 Effronites.
16 Socinians.
16 Interimists.
16 Libertines.
16 Farnovians.
16 Erquinians.
16 Schwenkfeldians.
16 Petro-brussians.
16 Stancarists.
16 Flacians.
16 Carolostadians.
16 Philipists.
16 Petro-joannites.
16 Osiandrians.
16 Alascani.
16 Arminians.
16 Synergists.
16 Ubiquitarians.
16 Autosiandrians.
16 Zwinglians.
16 Sub-Lapsarians.
16 Supra-Lapsarians.
16 Amsdorfians.
16 Galenists.
16 Majorists.
16 Lutherans.
16 Gomerists.
16 Hoffmanians.
16 Illuminati.
16 Independents.
16 Anabaptists.
16 Presbyterians.
16 Imperfect Mennonites.
16 Perfect Mennonites.
17 Antinomians.
17 Rosicrucians.
17 Ranters.
17 Beddelians.
General Baptist.
Particular "
17 Anti-Mission "

Church was organized by Christ." Such persons overlook the very gist of the whole matter. Christ Jesus is still on earth in His Body Mystical. Private judgment is all very well and proper so

17 Free-Will Baptist.
7th-Day "
6-Principle "
Scottish "
River Brethren.
Christian Connection.
Campbellites.
Winnebrenarians.
17 Borrelists.
17 Collegiants.
17 5th Monarchymen.
17 Drabicians.
17 Seekers.
17 Cocceians.
17 Se Baptists.
17 Muggletonians.
17 Bourignonists.
17 Crypto Calvinists.
17 Amyraldists.
17 Apostoolians.
17 Rogerines.
17 Cornarists.
17 Waterlandians.
17 Anti-Burghers.
17 Cameronians.
17 Haldanites.
17 Labadists.
17 Keithians.
17 Gortonians.
17 Lampetians.
17 Quakers.
Moravians.
Nicolites.
18 Inghamites.
18 Leadlyans.
18 Allenites.
18 Lifters, or New Lights.
18 Anti-Lifters, or Old Lights.
18 Reanointers.
18 Southcottians.
18 Hopkinsians.
18 Shaking Quakers.
18 Hattemists.
Scotch Presbyterian Seceders.
Original Seceders.
Old Light Seceders.
18 The Three Denominations.
18 Destructionists.
18 Free Thinkers.
18 Baxterians.
18 Sandemanians.
18 Dissidents.
18 Ellerians.
18 Separates.
18 Wilkinsonians.
18 Bereans.
18 Avignonists.
18 Disciplinarians.
18 Dunkers.
18 Daleites.
18 Calvinistic Methodists.
18 Wesleyan Methodists.
18 Swedenborgians.
18 New Connection Methodists.

RECENT.

Millerites.
Carbonari.
Hicksites.
Gurneyites.
Wilberites.
New School Presbyterians.
Old School Presbyterians.
United Presbyterians.
Associate Reformed Presbyterians.
Methodist Church, South, Black.
Methodist Church, South, White.
Cumberland Presbyterian.
United Synod of Presbyterian Church.
Mormons.
Methodist Reformers.
Primitive Methodist.
Central "
Independent "
Free "
Protestant "
Evang. Asso. "
Bryanites.
Whitefield Methodist, Tabernacle Connection.
Whitefield Methodist, Lady Huntington Connection.

long as God keeps silence. Let it have full reign. But when Jesus Himself speaks through His Body Mystical, it is time for private judgment to yield and be a little humble.

Whitefield Methodist, Welsh Calvinistic Connection.
Parkerites (?).
Irvingites.
Associate Synod of North America.
Associate Reform Synod of the South.
Free Presbyterian Synod.
Second Adventists.

BESIDES THE ABOVE.

Dutch Reformed.
Marcosians.
German Reformed Church.
Rellyan Universalists.
Monarchians.
Strigolniks.
Anti-Sabbatarians.
Unitarians.
Apostolics.
Universalists.
Restorationists.
Christians.
Halcyons.
Bonosians.
Caputiati.
Harmonists.
Lollards.
Ebadians.
Epefanoftschins.
Ortlibenses.
German Evang. Union.
Diaconoftschins.
Bezpopoftschins.
And others too numerous to mention.

Surely Sectarianism has tried often enough to found a lasting form of the Church.

VI.

CATHOLICITY AND ITS PRESENTMENT OF CHRISTIANITY, AS OPPOSED TO THE PRESENTMENT MADE BY PROTESTANTISM.

"Hold fast the form of sound words."—2 Tim. i. 13.

I resume the consideration of our main topic. The next step for us to take is to begin to develop what should be urged on the attention both of the masses and of the cultivated intellect of the day instead of Protestantism. What the world needs is neither Protestantism nor Rome, but Catholicity, the reasonable Catholic faith, the beautiful Catholic system, the warm, devoted, self-sacrificing Catholic spirit. What we want is less blind and foolish prejudice against Rome, that we may go to Her and learn why it is, and by what Catholic means it is, that She succeeds in all that in which She does succeed; and less prejudice in Rome against the real and legitimate advance of the nineteenth century (pardon the vagueness of this phrase), in order that She may learn why it is that She fails in some respects. We need more of the Catholic spirit of our Church brought out; Rome needs the errors which are merely accidental to Her system abolished, that we may both together move with crushing momentum, first upon the Protestant outworks, and then upon the infidel citadel itself. If Protestantism has lost its hold on the masses, Romanism has equally lost its hold on the intellect of the day. We want less preaching of generalities, about what is, after all, mere natural goodness, and more of positive, dogmatic teaching that shall be distinctively Christian.

Now, first, what is this Catholic faith that I speak of? The word "Catholic" means universal. Where am I to find that Catholic faith, then? Suppose I go to the Methodists and ask them for their "Faith" and its concomitants. They would tell me of the foreknowledge of God; they would point me to their class-meetings and their class-leaders. But I should look in vain for all this in Italy, in Russia, in Spain, in South America, in Austria. And I should soon discover that the Methodists were a mere local body. Suppose, then, I should go to the Presbyterians. They would tell me of Fore-ordination and Absolute Decree; they would point me to their ruling Elders and their Presbyteries. I should find all this different from Methodism. And, moreover, I should find that the Presbyterian was merely a local body also. Suppose I should go to the Quakers. They would point me to their want of sacraments and of an ordained ministry, and to their silent meetings. Here is something different still. Well, leaving all such, suppose I should come to our Church. She would point me, among other things, to her Thirty-nine Articles. I find that these are different from the Baptist or Congregational or Methodist declarations of faith. I should, moreover, look in vain for the Anglican Church *per se* in Sweden, in Brazil, or in Hungary. Suppose, then, I should go to the Roman Church. She would point me, among other things, to her Tridentine decrees and her Papal supremacy. But I should look in vain for all this through Russia or Siberia. I should find her also local as a body. It is clear I have gone the round world over and have not reached yet any faith that is Catholic. I find divisions in Christendom—schism. The complete set of dogmas and of corresponding practice, as presented by any one of these bodies, is not accepted by all the rest.

But now suppose it should happen that all Christendom to-day could agree in one faith, would you not call that the Catholic faith? I suppose you would. But, beloved, suppose that faith should happen to be different from the faith as held in mediæval times, or as held in the fourth or the first century, then it would not be the Catholic faith. For there are two kinds of schism, viz., the schism of space and the schism of time. In the Church of to-day one body of Christians may be cut off by schism from another. But schism may at least be conceived as equally existing between the entire body of Christians today, and the entire body in the eighth century, whereby the former body are cut off from the latter. And all schism is sin.

Thus you will see our faith may be local in time as well as in space. That only which has been held everywhere, always, and by all, is the Catholic faith. Here, then, we have reached our first approximation toward what we seek; that is to say, the Catholic faith is that which is held everywhere, always, and by all.

Now let us start on our second approximation. Is there any point, in Faith, Doctrine, or Practice, that has been agreed upon everywhere, always, and by all who call themselves Christians? Nothing under the sun. Justification? Churchmen differ from Lutherans. Election? Calvinists differ from Methodists. The Ministry? Baptists differ from Catholics. Sacraments? The Quakers do not have them. The Bible? Some hold to the whole, others only to a part. God Himself? Unitarians hold to one, Trinitarians hold to another. We would seem to be as far from what we want as ever. But not so far as it seems. For there is either a Catholic faith, or there is not; that is to say, there is *something* for man to rest in, or there is absolutely nothing. It were a most unreasonable supposition that God, after working out that splendid series of supernatural events which began in Abraham, continued through the acts of Moses, the organization of the typical Jewish Church, the foretellings of the prophets, the incarnation of His Son, His death and resurrection, the establishment of His Church, the descent of the Holy Ghost upon It, the continued existence of His Church, and all the magnificent events the latter involves—I say it would be a most unreasonable supposition that God, after all this, should have left man utterly at sea, with nothing definite to believe concerning it all. And, furthermore, it were equally unreasonable to suppose that, after God had thus acted definitely through a long series of centuries, and consistently unto some definite end, there would not be men all along through time, who, in their fallibility, their blindness, their ignorance, arrogance, or wilfulness, would fail to understand it all, and would misrepresent it either in its parts or as a whole. All men must be infallible in order for this not to happen. In the structure of affairs we are to anticipate that some men can be found, either in the past or present, who will deny any given part you please of the whole Divine movement. This only proves man's fallibility, not that there is no Catholic faith. Nay, God has not cast the most solemn and vital interests of man upon the rock of fallible private judgment. It is Satan that hath impaled them upon the sharp point of that rock and wrecked them. It were the wildest extravagance, therefore, were we not to limit the phrase "Everywhere, always, and by all," in some way, and so take our second legitimate approximation toward what we seek, namely—the Catholic faith. It were absurd, then, to look to all who call themselves Christians, if we would find the Catholic faith. The Catholic faith, then, is not the Christian faith as it may be held by this, that, or the other fallible man; but it is the faith as it has been held by the infallible Catholic Church.

We are forced, then, into the preliminary question, what is the Catholic Church? In answering this we shall be making our third and last approximation toward the Catholic faith. Where, then, shall I find the Catholic Church? Now, a church is an organism. The Catholic Church must be an organism universal over space and universal back through time to Christ. Suppose, now, I go to the Methodists again. I find there an organism; but in looking back I find it was arranged about the time of JOHN WESLEY, one hundred years ago. Before his day there was no such church organism. I pass then to the Presbyterians. There I find a different organism. But in looking back I find it dates its origin only about three hundred years ago. That will not answer, then. Very well, I try the Congregationalists, and, in fact, each and all of the modern Protestant organizations. Avowedly, they do not any of them run back into the dreadful mediæval times—those *dark* ages. Whatever these Protestant organisms may be, then, they must each and all be set aside as, at any rate, not Catholic organisms either in space or in time, and therefore not Catholic at all. Well, suppose I come to our Church. I find it, as an organism, with its bishops, priests, and deacons, its ritual form of worship, its altars and sacraments, its Conventions and Synods, its dioceses and parishes, running back in the history of England into mediæval times; yea, still farther back through the early days of old Britain and up even to the Apostles. I seem to strike something Catholic here. But be not in haste. Suppose I go to the Roman Church. I find that I can trace its life back also uninterruptedly to the Apostles. Suppose I go to the Greek Church. I find the same peculiarity of continued existence back to the Apostles there. Here, then, in the Roman, Greek, and Anglican Churches, we have reached something which it will do at least to pause upon for further investigation.

But have a care. When we look a little more closely into the Anglican organization as a whole, and consider it part by part, and when we examine the Roman organization in like manner, and the Greek, we find that each of the three differs from the other two in certain respects. Rome has a Pope and a cultus of St. Mary the ever-Virgin; these are not parts of the Greek or of the Anglican organisms. Though we have paused here, then, though the Catholic Church must be hereabouts somewhere, nevertheless, when we have reached our Church, we have not yet reached the

Catholic Church which we are in search of; when we go to Rome we have not yet reached that Catholic Church. And equally when we go to the Greeks we have not reached the object of our search. For we find that neither of these three organisms, when taken as a whole, and in all its minutiæ, is accepted by the other two. Shall we go elsewhere then? There is nowhere else to go. Let us look, then, more closely still here.

As we examine, we find that although the three, Anglican, Greek, and Roman, thus differ in some respects, they are marvellously alike in all others. All three have a hierarchy of Bishops, priests, and deacons. All have the Holy Altar of the Tremendous Sacrifice as the central object in their churches. All have robed clergy. All have Saints' days and identical Ecclesiastical Seasons. All have a ritual form of worship. All have parishes, dioceses, and provinces. All date their life back into the first century. All have stately ceremonials and processions; the Greeks the most glorious, the Romans less, and the Anglicans the least. All acknowledge the authority of General Councils. All have the same Apostolic Succession and the same Sacraments. Here, then, I begin to find the Catholic Church. Those few peculiarities in which the Greek, the Anglican, and the Roman differ from each other, are merely local; all those many peculiarities in which the three are at one, shape out for me visibly, solidly, and sharply the great Catholic Church; one in space as in organism, and one in time ; to be found equally in Russia, and Italy, and England, and America, and Mexico, and Germany, and Brazil —everywhere ; to be found, too, in the Nineteenth Century and equally in mediæval time, and also in the earliest days, unchanged and unchangeable. And every thing in the Anglican, Greek, and Roman bodies, which the three hold in common, and which has been held in them everywhere, always, and by all, is Catholic. Any thing else, any peculiarity which we have that Rome and the Easterns have not, or which Rome has but the Greeks and we have not, or which the Greeks have but Rome and we have not, is merely local, partial, and not Catholic.

I repeat, for years we have been talking about our Church as *the* Church; but what is that but mere high-and dry Anglicanism? It is not Catholicity. Equally so Rome has been calling herself *the* Church. *Pars pro toto.* But what is that but mere Romanism, not Catholicism? Just so the Greeks have called themselves *the* Church. As well might New York or New Jersey call itself the Middle States. There is a popular saying, "Rome or Reason." This is simply because people have identified Rome with Catholicity. But a part was never yet the whole. Christ never promised to be with a part of the Catholic Church to guide it into all truth, any more than He has promised to be with a single individual; it was only the whole Church Catholic He promised thus to be with. Rome's *dicta*, therefore, come to us with no binding authority. When the Whole Church speaks then will we yield, and then only, because then it will be Christ Jesus speaking. "Rome or Reason" is a snare to unwary souls. No, my friends; we deny that we must accept either Rome or Reason. But substitute in your alternative the word "Catholicity" for the word "Rome," and make it "Divine Catholicity," or "Human Reason," and we will take our stand just there, and join issue with you to the end.

Permit me to close this part of my discourse by an illustration of the Catholic Church. We will take, for the sake of simplicity, a tree. For eight feet above the soil its trunk stands one and entire. Somewhere along the ninth foot the trunk branches into two main limbs. We will call the Eastern the Greek limb, and the Western we will call the Latin. Six feet farther out on the Latin limb, that is to say, fifteen feet from the ground, that Western limb subdivides into two vast branches. The outmost of the two we will call the Anglican branch, the other we will call the Roman. These two branches and the Greek limb run up to a height of nineteen and a half feet from the ground. There they are, the three great boughs, each with its foliage, Anglican at the West, Roman in the centre, Greek at the East. If now you shield your vision from all but the top of the tree, there will appear to you to be three disconnected tufts of vegetation, but lo! the foliage and the flowers are the same. But remove now the shield from before your eyes, and behold in the whole tree a symbol of the Catholic Church—one organism from root to summit. A Church that is one like the trunk of that tree for the first nine centuries—that branches then into Eastern and Western; the Western subdividing at the fifteenth century into Anglican and Roman. As a fact the unity of the organism is not broken; intercommunion between its three parts is simply suspended for a time—suspended until that differentiation shall take place in God's One Church, which, as Herbert Spencer so admirably shows, is the law of all growth; a differentiation which means in its last issue, not a complete sundering of the parts, but the eventual unity of multiplexity, the harmony of coördinate parts. Did it not mix the metaphor somewhat, I would go on and complete the illustration by supposing sundry branches of this tree to be cut off from time to time, and inserted into vases of water standing round about the great tree. Being without root, those cut longest ago are all dead; while only the the most recently cut are green with a deceptive life, themselves soon to wither and die. These cut branches, standing trunkless and rootless about the living tree, would be apt symbols of the Protestant sects.

We have found, then, what the Catholic Church is. Now, the Catholic faith is the faith as held by that Catholic Church. "Faith" is different from "Doctrine." That which any one of the three limbs has as a peculiarity of its own, is not the Catholic faith. But all that which the three limbs have in common with each other, and in common with the trunk below even down to the roots, *that* is Catholic. What faith is it, then, that they all hold in common? Not the Thirty-nine Articles, for they are merely Anglican; not the Tridentine Decrees, for they are merely Roman; not the decrees of the Synod of Bethlehem, for they are merely Greek. But the faith as set forth by those great Councils wherein all three took part, wherein the whole Church spoke. The faith, namely, known as the Niceno-Constantinopolitan Creed, which all three to-day accept, and which the whole Church has from the first accepted, even before those councils set that faith in its present framework of words. Now, then, we are ready to answer the question, what is this faith? It is the *Catholic presentment of Christianity* involving a Church visible as a vital part of Christianity. It is fundamentally different from the Protestant presentment of Christianity. It is not a heterogeneous list of articles about justification, and the Bible as the rule of faith, and sanctification and election. It is organic as a whole; that is to say, each statement in it grows out of the preceding, and, in turn, opens the way for the one following. It is not a list of disconnected theological conclusions, hard to understand as Spinoza or Ralph W. Emerson. It is, on the other hand, a plain record of historic and other fact. It is simply the consecutive history of what God has done to save man, in order that every man may know what it is and freely take advantage of it. It is, in brief, a very clear description of the course which, in the Divine purpose, Grace takes as it starts from God the Father, and reaches at last the individual sinner.

Now let us examine and analyze it. It begins by giving us God the Father Almighty, Maker of all that is visible and invisible. Its second step is to give us God the Son, and the perfect unity subsisting between Father and Son in God. For the Son is "God of God, and of One Substance with the Father." Its third step is the statement that the Son came down to earth and became man, took our nature upon Him; and it gives us the perfect unity of Godhead and manhood in Jesus Christ; "came down from heaven, was incarnate, was made man." Its fourth step gives us the gradual perfecting of Christ's manhood by suffering: "He suffered, was crucified, was buried." Its fifth step gives us the resurrection and ascension of the perfected manhood, and the giving of the Holy Ghost to His Church. Its sixth step gives us the Holy Catholic and Apostolic Church. Its seventh gives us baptism into that Church. Its eighth gives us the remission of sins consequent upon that baptism. Its ninth, our resurrection. And its tenth and last, our life everlasting.

Now, what is all this, beloved? It is all a very awful matter; but it is all a very plain and easily understood matter nevertheless. It is simply Christianity as distinguished from Rationalism. Any thing less than or outside of it is Rationalism, even though it may surround itself with pulpits, and build meeting-houses, and have ministers, and services on Sundays, and read the Bible, and preach sermons to its votaries. It is simply and solely the history of what God has done to save you. It is, in short, the Gospel. It is simply and solely a consecutive record, a description of the course—that is to say, of the channel—which, in the Divine purpose, grace takes as it starts from God the Father, and at last reaches any individual sinner for his salvation.

For, first we have God the Father, the source of all things—the source, therefore, of that grace. Then, second, we have the Son and the Father, one in God; so that the grace in the Father flows out uninterruptedly and fills the Son, owing to their unity. This is the first step the grace reaches in its journey toward you and me. Then, third, Godhead and manhood in Jesus Christ are one; and after Christ's manhood is perfected through suffering, the grace in His Godhead flows out and fills His manhood owing to their unity: that manhood rising, ascending, and receiving the gifts for us. This is the second stage which the grace reaches in its journey from God the Father toward you and me, viz., into the man's nature, *i. e.*, the Soul and Body Natural of Christ. Then comes the Holy Catholic Church, the Body Mystical of Christ, which is one with His Body Natural. Scripture exhausts all metaphor to make us realize how entirely one are Christ and His Body Mystical, the Church. At Pentecost, the grace which filled His Body Natural in Heaven now flowed out and filled His Body Mystical, the Church, owing to their unity; it did not descend on individuals, as such, but on the Body of the Church. This is the third stage which the grace reaches in its journey from God the Father toward you and me. The Church on earth, the One, Holy, visible, organic, perpetual, Apostolic and Catholic Church is its great Reservoir; not any one part of it alone; not Rome alone, but the whole Church. Who tells *me*, then, that I must go to Rome, when, as an Anglican, I am already in the Catholic Church! Why, I simply laugh at his want of comprehension. The Catholic Church is the Reservoir on earth. But how is that grace to reach and fill you, poor sinner? The Catholic creed goes on to tell you: You, as an individual, must become as one with that Church, or Body Mystical of Christ, as It is with His Body Natural, as the latter is with His Godhead, which is one with the Father. This is the last unity in the Gospel of salvation. How is this last unity to be effected? The very next step in the creed tells you. You must acknowledge the one baptism, and take advantage of it for yourself and for your children with hallelujahs, for the grace will now have reached its last designed stage, viz., the individual, to work spiritual health in him.

This is the plain history of the whole matter. This alone gives any sanction to baptism. This alone lifts it from the status of a mere empty form. The Catholic Faith then goes on to tell you of the Communion of all the Saints together in the grace, who are thus made one by baptism with the Church, with Christ, with God. Then the Creed proceeds as a consequence to tell you of the forgiveness of their sins. And as death is by sin, death being the sundering of body from soul, the Creed gives next, what is consequent upon the remission of sin, namely, the resurrection of the body; and closes, coming to its climax, by stating the object of all this, namely, your life everlasting.

Now, this is the Catholic faith. This is the presentment made to the world by the Catholic Church, everywhere, always, and by all, of Christianity as a *mediatorial* system. God the Father and the sinner are put wide apart by sin. They are to be reconciled—are to be brought to an *at-one-ment.* Something comes in between to do this. That is what *mediation* means; something coming in between; and *that,* not to sunder, but to unite. That which comes in between the sinner and God the Father must be real and operative, and not a mere intellectual conception. It must be something that literally grasps hold of us, not a mere idea which we grasp and contemplate. Now, what is this mediatorial operation, that, in God's purposes, comes in between and lays hold of us that we may be saved? Why, who is the great Mediator? It is Jesus Christ. But Jesus Christ must not be a mere intellectual idea which we can be thankful for. As a Mediator He must be operative. And how does Christ operate as a Mediator? Why, through His Body Mystical and its extensions (its arms, so to speak), which are one with Himself, just as I operate through my body natural which is one with me. At the very first, in Palestine, Christ came and operated in His body Natural; He walked and spoke in it; but ever since then, and out over the earth, and down through the centuries, He walketh and speaketh and doth operate through His Body Mystical. The extensions of that Body Mystical are the Ministry and the Sacraments. All this (that is to say, Christ Jesus, not as a mere intellectual idea, but Christ and *all of Him*) is the Mediator; which speaks to the sinner to-day and every day, "I pray you be reconciled to God;" and which then lays hold of the willing but helpless sinner by Baptism, and makes him one with the Divine Life, setting him in It like a graft into a tree, and then feeds him with the Divine Life through the Blessed Eucharist. All this, I say, is what the Catholic Faith declares to be "Christianity, the Doctrine of Mediation." Now, all other systems, which deprive Christ of His Body Mystical, which preach a half-Christ and not the whole Christ, which preach a broken, bruised, mutilated Christ, which cut off from Him the Apostolic Ministry and Sacraments, that are the very arms by which through the centuries and all over the earth He mercifully lays hold of and folds sinners into at-*one*-ment with Himself and the Father, and feeds them with His Life, all other, that is to say, all Protestant schemes, are but schemes of incipient Rationalism, which have so wounded the Gospel truth and fact of Mediation, that it soon dies of the wounds it has received even in the house of its Protestant friends. All the nursing, all the anxiety, all the watchings of Protestant, Calvinist and Armenian, will not save the doctrine of Christian Mediation, after it is thus mutilated, from sinking into the death of Unitarianism. The Catholic Gospel of salvation is simple. Be baptized into the Church, for that Church Catholic is one with Christ, and Christ is one with the Father. Of course, I need not qualify this statement by saying, that it supposes the baptized man will faithfully use the Means of Grace made over to him by God through the Church. The whole is summed up in this, viz.: "The union of God and man, begun in the person of Christ, is continued and extended in the Church, which is the Body of Christ; the Church acting through its Ministry and Sacraments."

I have but time to contrast in a word the

Protestant Gospel of salvation with all this. The Protestant is told to stand outside of this really operative work of Mediation, and to agonize as an individual until an "ictus falls from behind the stars," until grace comes in the fashion of an invisible streak of lightning out of the far Heaven, and pierces his individual breast. But is this *Mediation?* Is this *Christianity?* What is it, after all, but the sheerest *Immediation* between the individual and God? And, brethren, no subjective intellectual notion which the individual may, at the same time, hold in his brain about Christ as some historic and distant being, who did something to make Himself somehow a Mediator, will save it from its Immediation. When you set a hard practical fact against a mere intellectual idea, the fact is always too much for the idea, and eventually drives it off, and holds the whole field to itself. And this is one reason why Protestantism invariably gravitates down into Unitarianism and avowed Rationalism. Now, these people have the supposed fact of a practical system of Immediation between God and the individual working all the time; what wonder if their *mere notion* of mediation vanishes at last before the stern reality, and they all sink, victims of Satan, into a denial at last of every thing distinctively Christian? What is Protestantism, then, but Rationalism—the system of Immediation, concealed in a Christian cloak. It is my part, as your pastor, watching for your souls, to strip off that cloak and show the demon within.

I have spoken of the Catholic Faith as being the Faith as held by the Catholic Church. I have described to you what that Faith is. It is perhaps not from the purpose of my subject to remind you that, besides the Faith as set down in the Creed, there is much else that is common to the Catholic Church. Her universal yearning for the faithful dead; Her universal prayers for their joyful resurrection—that they "may have their perfect consummation and bliss, both in body and soul, in God's eternal and everlasting glory;" "Remember not, Lord, our offences, nor the offences of our forefathers;" "Most humbly beseeching Thee to grant that, by the merits and death of Thy Son Jesus Christ, and through faith in His Blood, we and *all Thy whole Church* may obtain remission of our sins, and *all other* benefits of His Passion;" Her universal love for the Saints; Her universal realization of the presence of Angels, not only round about Her altars at the Eucharist, but round about us as guardians, to "be our succor and defence on earth;" Her universal tenderness for the confessing penitent; Her universal declarations of absolution—"Receive ye the Holy Ghost," the Anglican Church says to each of Her priests at ordination, "whose sins thou dost forgive, they are forgiven; and whose sins thou dost retain, they are retained;"—the separateness that marks and the glory that surrounds universally Her altars. People sometimes say, when they enter one of our churches, "Why, it looks like a Roman Catholic church!" As a matter of course, beloved; why should it not? It is not intended that two brothers should not look at least *like* each other. It were very strange if they did not. Still, brethren, do not identify a gorgeous ritual, befitting the presence of our tremendous Sacrifice Christ Jesus, with a Roman ritual. The Anglican is not the Roman Church, though both are Catholic. Two brothers, though they may be *alike*, are by no means the *same*. There are points in Rome which She has added to the Catholic system, but which we, as Anglicans, and which equally the Greeks, are uncompromisingly opposed to, which belong not to this age, and which must be abolished before intercommunion can take place. But, nevertheless, a gorgeous ritual is in itself Catholic, and, so long as it symbolizes the Catholic verities, and no Roman errors, is surely in harmony with our Church as a visible and symbolic Body. While we do not propose to be Roman, we do not hesitate, not only to be, but even to seem to be, Catholic. Like Lazarus, our Church has been bound in the grave-clothes of Protestantism and prejudice; but the Lord, Her loving Master, hath come, and, as Her Marys and Her Marthas stand weeping, He calls Her forth, and utters the glad mandate, "Loose Her, and let Her go!"

Before I close, perhaps I may be pardoned if

I say a word or two touching the able leading article in the *Daily World*, the ingenious communication in the same journal signed "Roman Catholic," and the leading article in the *Christian Observer*. Long-settled prejudices and cherished feelings are never touched by hostile hand without danger of exciting passion and vituperation. And I desire to express in some public way my obligations for the calm and manly spirit shown by each of the three writers. Of course, it is not my purpose, during the delivery of these sermons, to answer editorial articles and anonymous newspaper correspondence. There would be no end to the discussion. Still, with your permission, I will reserve to myself the privilege of lingering a moment for a brief remark on each of the articles mentioned above.

The *World* admits the first main charge in the first sermon, namely, that Protestantism has failed to reach the masses. It declines, perhaps very properly, to take the responsibility of deciding one way or the other as to whether Protestantism leads logically to infidelity, which was our second main charge. It says, however, that, if Protestantism "be not in the condition of the Church of Sardis and the Church of the Laodiceans," as those Churches are depicted in the third chapter of Revelation, "it is time they proved it;" and that "silence and inaction are no longer safe for them." The only remedy which the *World* suggests for the evils charged is, for each large parish to sell its church and land, and, with the proceeds, build several inexpensive churches, one of which shall be for its own use, and the others to be free to all comers. I have only to remark on this, that it is an admirable and Catholic suggestion, full of common sense; but that, nevertheless, I fail to see how it would touch the real difficulty. For, after all, it would be the self-same old Protestantism that would be preached in those free churches, which, as a concealed Rationalism, has been abandoned for the genuine article by the Intellect of the Age, and which has disgusted the masses for many reasons besides its abominable system of "hired pews."

The writer signing himself "Roman Catholic" also admits the gravity of the charges. But he claims that the Rationalism of the day is not the logical result of Protestantism *per se*, but only of its Lutheranism and its Calvinism; and the cure he suggests is, for Protestantism to discharge Lutheranism and Calvinism out of itself. This is just precisely what I claim the Intellect of the Age has been doing; and lo, the phenomenon—with Lutheranism and Calvinism emptied out, you have no Protestantism left! Thus, it seems to me, the cure kindly suggested by "Roman Catholic" is, to kill the patient. Terrible satirist, he sees the point!

The editor of the *Christian Observer* first denies the charge that German, English, Swiss, and New-England Rationalism is the outgrowth of

Protestantism. He then attempts to prove this denial by asserting that Romanism also has made infidels in Italy and France. I do not deny the latter fact; indeed, I have expressly stated it. But I fail to see how Romanism leading to infidelity proves that Protestantism does not. Suppose that I should assert that sugar-coated strychnine kills, and you attempt to prove that it will not by asserting that something else will—why, I should simply have nothing to say in reply. As for the balance of this paragraph of the article under notice, I am not disposed to take an undue advantage: it was evidently written in haste. I simply leave the writer to the tender mercies of his sarcastic friend, "Roman Catholic." If "Roman Catholic" can prove that the *Observer* is wrong, then so much the worse for the *Observer;* if not, then so much the better for me and the Anglican Catholic Church. The editor of the *Observer* then goes on to deny that the Roman Catholic Church reaches the masses. I might leave him to settle this point with the *Daily World.* But I will at least say that he has, perhaps, forgotten that when the mob raged through our streets, defying all the power of police and soldiery, the lifted finger of the Archbishop calmed and dispersed it in an hour. He has, perhaps, forgotten that every one of the six, eight, or ten Masses said at every Roman Catholic Church of a Sunday morning is thronged with worshippers, and every mass with a different congregation. "But," the editor goes on to say, "how much better are the crowds for it?" That's not for me to say. If his insinuation be correct, then *that* is a difficulty between "Roman Catholic" and him. I've got nothing to do with it. My point is, that, whether for good or for evil, Rome gets at the masses, and Protestantism does not, and cannot, either in Romish or in Protestant lands. And precisely for this reason, namely, that Rome presents to the masses the real Christ, and so goes to them with authority, while Protestantism presents them with a mere intellectual notion about Christ; and the "authority," instead of being on the side of Protestantism as she approaches the masses, is avowedly on the side of the private judgment of the masses, which may reject that intellectual notion or not. "How much better are the masses for all Rome?" cries the *Observer*. It never suggested itself to the *Observer* to ask, how much worse the masses might be but for Rome. The editor then proceeds to show how Protestantism gets at the masses. "Look at all your organized benevolence," cries he; "the organized benevolence of New York is a fruit of Protestantism." The coolness of this statement is somewhat admirable. "Private Judgment," and "Every man his own Priest," and "Divine Foreknowledge," and "Final Perseverance," and "Infant Damnation," the cause of all the organized benevolence of New York! Perhaps there are no human hearts underneath doubting heads in the city of New York; perhaps there are no natural tender sympathies; perhaps there are not hundreds and hundreds of merchants who never enter a church from one month's end to another, but who yet put their hands in their pockets constantly, and pour out thousands at the call of want. Perhaps, forsooth, Protestantism is responsible too for all the deeds of charity that were done in ancient Greece and Rome. And then again, perhaps, there are no vast hospitals, and asylums, and homes in this city belonging to the Roman Church. "The organized benevolence of New York is how Protestantism goes down to the masses," cries the *Observer*. Even should I admit that Protestantism, *per se*, is the mother of any organized benevolence, there is still the heavy charge behind, that, while it is mending legs, it is losing souls. The *Observer* comprehends my position, and I respect the ability it has displayed in fighting for a losing cause; but I do not know that I have any thing in particular to say concerning the Baltimore *Episcopal Methodist*, or the *Protestant Churchman*, the New-York *Methodist*, or the Philadelphia Roman Catholic *Universe*, and so I pass on. I trust *you* will not fall into the popular error of thinking that electricity or the sewing-machine is Protestantism.

What the world needs, I repeat, is neither the sugar-coated strychnine of Protestantism, nor the strychnine-coated sugar of Romanism, but Catholicity, the Catholic faith, and the Catholic system, and the Catholic spirit.

All this opposition to a return to this Catholic faith and spirit and customs, all this struggle, for instance, against one of the mere symptoms of returning health, namely, the clothing of worship with its fitting splendor, is but the old story of Mrs. Partington and her broom. Some persons are anxious that canons be passed to stop ritual. If such canons be passed, of course they will be obeyed. But it is quite immaterial whether they are passed or not. If not, then the stream with its ever-gathering waters will flow. If passed, then such canons will only be a dam in the way, and there will be a gathering of the floods behind it, which, in God's good time, will sweep off and utterly away both the dam and they that guard it. So futile is it to attempt to stem the purposes of Almighty God.

VII.

REPLY TO STRICTURES IN THE RELIGIOUS PRESS AND FROM THE PULPIT.

"And many false prophets shall rise, and shall deceive many."—MATT. xxiv. 11.

THE articles and sermons purporting to be replies, either direct or indirect, to the charges made from this place against Protestantism, are so extraordinary as to demand at least brief notice. Six weeks have now passed, but, although there has been a very manifest uneasiness among the Puritans, and a good deal written and said, it is almost needless to remark, not a solitary charge has been met, nor a solitary argument answered. The first canon which reviewers should observe is, to understand that which they are attempting to criticise.

Three distinct charges have been made, viz.: As a religious system, Protestantism fails to get at the masses; nay, there were vast regions of country where its fundamental principles (to wit, private judgment, and the dogma of a church invisible only) took deep and general root; but in those countries it has absolutely lost its hold on the masses it once swayed; therefore it is a failure. Secondly—The logical issue of Protestantism is Rationalism, i. e., Protestantism logically destroys Christianity; therefore it is a failure, and, worse, it is a delusion, a snare to souls, a heresy. Thirdly—In the lands where it has prevailed, as in Germany, parts of Switzerland, New England, and elsewhere, the historical event has substantiated the logical anticipation; for those lands are to-day honeycombed with infidelity; therefore Protestantism is a failure, and people should wake up to the fact, abandon it, and look for something better. To these charges I have added the subordinate statement that Rome also has failed in some respects; but I assert that Her failures are not on account of Her Catholicity, since they can be traced directly to those very points where She has perverted the ancient Catholicity, or overlaid it with foreign and incongruous peculiarities. Catholicity is divine; and experience shows us that it suits all centuries, that it is adapted to and can co-exist harmoniously with every form of political government, from the absolute monarchy to the republic, and with every degree of enlightenment, from the lowest to the highest. Romanism, on the other hand, is human in its origin; it sprang in some of its features out of the necessities of the Middle Ages and their feudalism, and is not in harmony with modern conditions and our advancing intelligence.

Now, these three charges against Protestantism have not been met; and, if I am to judge by letters from perfect strangers, of which I am daily in receipt, the public are beginning to see that they have not been met, and to inquire what the matter is. Protestants cannot turn this important subject aside with a mere wave of the hand, and a vain attempt to prove that electricity is Protestantism. The subject is one of too deep moment for this. It is squarely up before the public, and unprejudiced people are thinking about it. Silence is dangerous; and these pretended replies, whether direct or indirect, that do not touch the real matter at issue, are fatal. They only exhibit the weakness of the cause.

Here, then, are the three distinct charges. How do these answerers and defenders of Protestantism meet the solemn issue? Why, all of them in one way. First, by showing that Rome has failed. Of course She has failed. But what has that to do with the charges? That is a difficulty between Rome and them; not between us and them. We have stated that the Roman Catholic Church is a failure in so far as She is Roman, and there we leave Her. We set up Catholicity for the cure, not Rome. But the difficulty with these men is, that they do not seem to comprehend that there is any other kind of Christianity except Protestantism and Romanism; and they think that, if we say Protestantism fails, we mean, of course, that everybody should take to

Rome. They do not comprehend that there is a third presentment of Christianity, viz., Catholicity, with nothing distinctively Roman in it, and nothing distinctively "Protestant" either. The fact is, that, what with Rome and what with Protestantism, God's old Catholicity has been under a cloud, and has not gained the general ear of the people in America. But they are beginning at last to arouse to it, and to understand it, if their leaders do not. This agitation is starting inquiry among new thousands, and the day is not distant when many more even than now will say to these answerers, "Your tirades against Romanism will not do; you do not meet the point; you must give us something different from that, if you expect to command our respect, to say nothing of our convictions." I will tell you, brethren, what the matter is: The difficulty is, the solemn charges cannot be met; they are too patent for denial, hence all this anger and floundering.

Then, secondly, attempt is made to identify Protestantism with the Nineteenth Century, and to palm that identification off as an answer. "Look at all the light of to-day," say they; "the commerce, the arts, the arms, the battle of Sadowa, the Spanish Revolution! Why, here is a man that calls all that a failure!" But, brethren, it will not do. Nobody has charged that the Nineteenth Century is a failure. Protestantism is not the Nineteenth Century. No one has charged that the needle-gun is a failure, or the sewing-machine, or the steamboat. The charge is not that the Nineteenth Century is a failure, but that something that *exists in* the Nineteenth Century has failed. No one has charged that freedom is a failure. On the contrary, the distinct assertion is made that true Catholicity, in the days of Henry VIII., rose against Rome in the interest of freedom, struck down Her Papal tyranny over political government, and Her tyranny over the intellect. And, by the way, the Anglican Church is to-day declaring its independence also of Protestant tyranny; and in England the tyrant Protestantism is mobbing Her for it. The liberty of Puritanism is to-day just what it was in Roger Williams's time, viz., perfect liberty for every one to believe just as the Puritan believes, or take the consequences. I tell you, my friends, we have liberty in spite of, and not because of, Protestantism. A man is at liberty to break down Christianity so long as he does so on the Protestant principle of private judgment, but a man is not at liberty to defend Christianity on Catholic principles. If he dares to, it is in the midst of angry scowls, social excision, and Protestant mobs.

But, to return—the distinction is, that in the Sixteenth Century true Catholicity struck for a true and guarded freedom in religion, while Protestantism struck for a ruinous license in religion. The charge is, that that license is a failure; that it hath wrecked the Bible, the Church, the Ministry, the Sacraments, and the Apostolic Faith. Within the wide, unalterable walls of that Faith there is a vast, almost a fearful, freedom touching doctrine allowed by God's Catholicity. Freedom in government, in thought, in action, is as dear to Catholicity as it is to any one. But the charge is, that that rampant license of Scripture interpretation, whereby the most ignorant are egged on to rush in where angels dare not tread, is an awful mistake, and has ended in the ruin of thousands of souls. This identification of the Nineteenth Century with Protestantism, which came out of the less-enlightened Sixteenth, and which is one of the mere accompaniments of modern times, will not do; and the public are seeing it, and saying it. Why, do these men really mean to assert that not only modern times, but every thing in modern times, is a success? that there have been no mistakes made in religion, in philosophy, in any thing? that modern times, forsooth, are immaculate? that our fathers and we are infallible? that Protestantism, because it belongs to modern times, is a success? Their fallacy proves too much; for then is the Comtean School of Positivism a success; then is Emersonian Pantheism a success; then is Spiritualism, and Parkerism, and Fourierism, and Mormonism, and Agrarianism, a success.

But, thirdly, these answerers, still avoiding the charges, attempt to cloud the matter by leading the public to suppose that Protestantism is the cause of all the glories of the Nineteenth Century. What! the religious dogma that says, "Away with God's Apostolic Visible Church, and let every man be his own Church, his own priest, his own interpreter of the Bible, and his own judge as to what the Bible is, or whether there is any Bible at all," that fatal religious dogma the cause, forsooth, of all this science and modern light? My brethren, it will not do; and people are seeing that, too, and saying it. But, if Protestantism be not the cause, do you ask me, what is? The real cause of the light and advance of modern times is not a theological dogma. But it is a general awakening of mind, which began far back in the middle ages, four hundred years before the Protestant dogma was ever thought of—an awakening of mind, of taste, of the genius of invention, which, abandoning the rude structures of the Seventh, Eighth, Ninth, and Tenth Centuries, brought out, long before the Continental Reformation, the most ornate specimens of architecture the world ever saw; which, in the Eleventh Century, invented paper, and, before John Calvin and Martin Luther ever saw the light, produced the art of printing—paper and printing, the two conservers of human intelligence; which, in the Twelfth Century, devised banks of exchange and discount, and not long after invented gunpowder, conceived the idea of the post-office, and discovered and applied the principle of magnetism in the mariner's compass thus giving such a start to commerce and magnificent geographical discovery as they had never had before; which, in the Tenth Century, contrived clocks; which invented painting in oil-colors before Luther was born; which, in the Thirteenth Century, introduced astronomy and geometry into Europe, and not long after brought in algebra, and fostered all three sciences; which discovered America a quarter of a century before the Continental "Reformation," so called, opened; which, centuries before Luther, produced a Dante, and a Petrarch, and a Chaucer, and a Boccaccio, and a Roger Bacon—Roger Bacon, who, three centuries before his successor, Lord Francis Bacon, announced to the world the very method of legitimate investigation in accordance with which all modern science is pursued, and upon which Lord Bacon afterward built his fame—Roger Bacon of the so-called dark ages, who had this immense advantage over the Bacon of the Sixteenth Century, in that he personally put his method into practice.

But I will pause. The cause of the light and advance of modern times was a general awakening of mind in Western Europe, which began clear back in the Tenth Century; which brought out all this that I have mentioned and more; which has been bringing out new blessings to man ever since; which has rolled out and up a thousand things—most of them good, some of them bad; which rolled up, after a while, the Protestant dogma for one of its many and varied productions; and which is rolling up to-day the solemn presentment of that dogma and of its fruits at the bar of this enlightened century, that they may be put on their trial.

And now these answerers are trying to make people think that this Protestantism is not one of the heterogeneous mixture of things that awakening mind, in its power but also in its fallibility, turned up (and *that*, four hundred years after awakening mind had begun to produce its marvellous fruits), but that it is, forsooth, the underlying cause of all the good of modern times—gunpowder, glass, paper, printing, painting, telescopes, astronomy, algebra, *Magna Charta*, and every thing else; —a mother producing children before she was born! Protestantism was but one of the effects of the general awakening of mind, not its cause; and our charge is, that it happened to be one of the bad effects—not in that it struck at Roman error, but because it sought to destroy Catholic truth also. Why, brethren, awakening mind must have been infallible not to have made at least some few mistakes. Let these gentlemen meet the charge, and not try to escape by raising a cloud of issues, which are so clearly false and foreign to the subject, that they are beginning to be remarked as such.

"Where Protestantism prevails, there every thing prevails which blesses mankind," it is said. Nay, it should have been said, that where awakened mind prevails, there thousands of things prevail which bless mankind, and some things which are not blessings. Where *Protestantism* prevails, indeed! Why, you might as well say where Spiritualism prevails, or Unitarianism, there every thing prevails which blesses mankind, and think that you have proved thereby that Spiritualism is a success; you might as well say where infidelity prevails, every thing prevails that blesses mankind, and think you have proved that infidelity is a success. For infidelity prevails throughout lands that once were Protestant, and in those lands the skeptics very much outnumber the believers.

And now for a very subordinate point in the connection. It is charged that Rome has opposed the advance of science; that Copernicus was excommunicated, and Galileo imprisoned. That is all true, and so much the worse for Rome, say we. That is something she must settle. But the inference intended to be drawn is, that Protestant religionists have been great friends of science. I do not say that true Catholics have been blameless in the premises either. But at any rate, it would be a little queer if those who hurl this missive at Rome should be found dwelling in houses of glass in this very year 1868. Ask Herbert Spencer, and Max Müller, and John Stuart Mill, and Darwin, and Lyell, and Huxley, and Professor Tyndall, and they will tell you—(some of them, indeed, have said, to an acquaintance of mine), that they get from Protestant religionists nothing but opposition in their efforts to unearth new scientific truth; and that their only sympathizers in the religious world are minds that have been trained in the Anglo-Catholic Church. When it was announced that the "world was round and like a ball," Rome resisted. When it was announced that "the earth moved round the sun," Rome resisted. When it was announced that "the world was not made in six natural days," Protestantism resisted, and said it was an infidel statement. When it was announced that "the flood could not have covered the whole earth," where was Protestantism? Why, her divines were resisting. She didn't shut the bold scientists up in prison, for that had gone out of fashion. But she did the nearest thing to it that she could. And now, to-day, when Darwin tells us that "Creation was and is by development," where are the overwhelming majority of Protestant divines? Why, in the opposition, denouncing Darwin. When Lyell and De Perthes tell us "man has existed one or two hundred thousand years," where are these Protestant divines that are such friends of science? Protestant religionists stand to-day in the attitude of open resistance to the advance of science, and centuries hence the finger of History will be pointed at them, as they to-day justly point the finger at Rome. It is even so, friends; we have liberty in spite of and not because of the spirit of Protestant religionists. Liberty in religion, liberty in government, liberty in speech, in thought, in the press, we have it because of awakening mind and not because of that spirit which Protestantism seems to create among men. Rome and Protestantism are equally tyrants. It is awakening mind that has been fighting for its rights on the domain both of doctrine and of science; yes, and of political government too, ever since the Tenth Century. All the way along from the Tenth to the Fifteenth Century it fought Rome, and all the way down from the Fifteenth to the Nineteenth it has been fighting Protestantism. When Protestantism threw off Roman tyranny, she only brought in another tyranny—a doctrinal tyranny. You must believe thus and thus as to the atonement, and justification, and regeneration, and election, or you are out of the pale of the Gospel. As I have sat by the dying bed of a sweet spirit that had, for years, been filled with the love of God and the love of man, but had known little of theology, and as I have heard, from those standing around, the metaphysical Protestant doctrine and the rigid notion pressed, and as I have seen the dying man turning his eyes from one to another, annoyed—made timorous at the edge of life—anxious to do right—striving to apprehend in accordance with the iron dogma, I have felt how cutting and galling were the chains of all this doctrinal tyranny which Protestantism brought in.

The Continental Reformation, with all its

claimed liberty, was born with the spirit of intolerance in it, and that spirit has marked its career ever since. Its intolerance began in that violent man Luther, a man who uttered such language concerning most sacred things as cannot be repeated to ears polite. I know that Reformers are made out of rugged material; that they are always tough men to meet. But that is neither here nor there so far as our point is concerned. Thus its intolerance began. It continued in Calvin, than whom a more tyrannical spirit can hardly be conceived. It slew Mary Queen of Scots, Strafford, and Laud, and martyred Charles the First. It went in the Puritans to Holland, and was so cross-grained there that when it sailed away the Dutchmen praised God for the merciful deliverance. It took ship and threatened to come to New York, and would have landed here had not the citizens found means to bribe the captain of the Mayflower to land his uncomfortable freight by mistake somewhere else. In Cromwell it would not be content to enjoy its own Congregationalism quietly; no, but it broke into the Church of England; it stripped off the garments from our clergy; with axes and hammers it broke down our carved work. It hanged witches. It drove out Roger Williams from its settlements into the inhospitable forests of Rhode Island for the liberty of belief which he claimed. In the Quakers it would not be content to enjoy silent meetings, but must go in and disturb the Puritan meetings with not only violent but even indecent behavior. And then, turning round, in the Puritans it hanged the Quakers. In the eighteenth century it pelted John Wesley through the streets and broke up his meetings. In the nineteenth century it mobs our priests while at their solemn services in the east of London; and as for our Sisters of Mercy, for the crime those gentle women have been guilty of in devoting themselves to lives of charity and prayer, to watchings in pestilential hospitals, it attacks them in the streets with missiles 'till they fly for their lives. Every mail from England brings us accounts of the tyranny and intolerance of Protestantism; while in America, not content with staying in its own houses of worship, it goes out of its way into one of ours, and as the priest stands performing his function at the altar, it speaks out in feminine tone of voice, so loud as to be heard for four or five pews around, "I would like to bang that man's back with my parasol." I tell you, my friends, we have liberty, and always have had it, in spite of and not because of Protestantism.

Some of my beloved brethren, who entirely agree with me, regret that I have used the word "Protestantism." They would have preferred "Sectarianism." But we never can cure that word "Protestant" of the general meaning it conveys to nine minds out of ten; that is to say, opposition not only to all that is Roman in Roman Catholicism, but also to all that is distinctively Catholic, both in the Roman and Anglican

Churches. The vast majority use the word "Protestant" in that sense, and so its meaning is fixed. When, therefore, we apply the word to ourselves, we apply it in a non-natural sense. And what is the use of our perpetually using it for ourselves and perpetually explaining our peculiar meaning of it to persons who will not understand? The word is a hopeless case. Let the sects have it—particularly as we are a Catholic Church.

Some of my brethren regret that I have spoken so plainly. We want peace, say they. Ah, what we want is not peace but truth. "But," say they, "you will frighten away some." My friends, we have pursued this timid policy too long. While we have been trying to lure the few easily-frightened ones into the Church by reticence, that reticence has been standing by and allowing thousands to go down *en masse* into infidelity. Besides, let the lines be drawn. Let the world understand that we are not with the Protestant sects. Until we do this frankly, our sister Churches of the Catholic world cannot be expected to look upon us with other than a suspicious eye; nor (what is of vast importance) will we be in position to command their attention and respect, as we stand our ground, and demand of them to modify their local systems—to cast off their errors to such extent as will enable a restoration of intercommunion. We are twenty millions; let us be true to ourselves, and we shall, if not in this century, perhaps in the next, be the means of reforming the whole Catholic Church.

VIII.

THE LATE PRACTICAL ADMISSIONS OF THE FAILURE OF PROTESTANTISM, BY PROTESTANTS THEMSELVES.

From what has been said and printed during the past week,* some of it having been written with direct reference, and some of it having been publicly said, without any reference (at least any avowed reference) to what has been laid before you from this place, I suppose there are many of you who regard the first campaign of the war as about closed. Still it may not be without interest to look a little at the results.

During the week a National Christian Convention of Protestant divines and laymen assembled in this city, and were in session several days. Some of their proceedings are of interest to us in this connection. In noticing these proceedings, I will not recapitulate the charges that have been

* These Discourses were preached in Christ Church, New York, during October and November, 1868. This closing Sermon was delivered on the evening of the last Sunday after Trinity (November 22), 1868.

made against Protestantism. I trust to your memories. But with regard to those charges, it seems that, whatever may have been urged in the past few weeks against our position, Protestants themselves have already been arousing to the sad truth of what we have charged. For, why was this Convention held? It was to discuss ways and means for the cure of evils. What were some of those evils? We will see anon. The Convention presented the melancholy spectacle of a body of people guilty of a mistake, awakening to the results of that mistake, but utterly oblivious that those results were directly traceable to fundamental errors inherent in the system to which they still cling; utterly oblivious to the fact that the evils, to discuss which they met, have not resulted from the bad application of a good system, but from the untiring application of a bad system.

Let us see what their circular letter convening the body says. I will not read it all, only extracts. The object of the Convention was, it seems, to consider, among other things, "*the indifference of the multitudes to the claims of the Gospel;*" "*the organized forms of attack on the authority of God's word;*" "*the inroads of an infidel philosophy reared upon the foundation of universal skepticism.*" And the circular goes on to say that the utmost energy is demanded, "*lest the high vantage-ground God has so graciously given His people in this country be stolen from them.*"

Well, there it is; what more, pray, can we ask? Whether with any reference to us or not makes no difference, the truth of the main charges, every one of them, is admitted in an official document of a national Protestant body. And several hundred of the leaders convene to see what can be done about it. Notwithstanding all that has been said against us, here is the ugly fact that Protestants are alarmed; that they are arousing to the truth that they have lost their hold both upon the intellect and upon the masses of the day; they feel that both are slipping away from them, and that *peculiar vigilance is demanded on their part lest they utterly lose the vantage-ground they once had entirely.* Indeed, beloved, it is a very noteworthy fact that both Rome and Protestantism have lost the *men* of the day. Their adherents are mostly women. There must be an intellectual feebleness about both systems. And there is another very noteworthy fact, that wherever true Catholicity has been brought out it gains more men than women. I do not say that women are not susceptible to it. In the end there is no doubt that the masculine and the feminine elements of its adherents will be equalized, but at present more men surrender to it than women. The fact is, whatever we may say of the women of the day, there are thousands of men left outside the walls of any faith, who cannot accept Protestantism, which they have shaken off, who will not surrender their proper freedom of thought to Rome, but who are craving for a faith of some kind—for a Christianity with reality, robustness, and common sense in it.

But let us see a little more about the action of this Convention. In discussing the first question that was up, the Rev. Dr. J. T. Duryea said that "whereas the Saviour had laid the command on His disciples to go and preach the Gospel to every creature, Christian people *were beginning to realize the startling fact* that the Gospel was not presented to every creature. It was not presented to the masses in this city. And he said that proportionately the Gospel was not presented to the masses as much in the country as in the city. Something was wrong." Comment were unkind and unnecessary. We pass on.

You will remember that the Church is large in England and very small in New England. Her Catholicity has been brought out more and more during the last thirty years in England, but until recently her Catholicity has been very little brought out in large sections of New England. Now what did the Rev. Dr. Hall and others say in the Convention? Why, when somebody called for missionary effort in England and Germany, Dr. Coy said, "Germany is full of infidelity," and Dr. Hall, saying nothing about Germany, leaving the claim all right for that, "insisted that *New* England needed more missionary work than Old England," and he "bewailed the unconverted state of New England." Ah, what a falling off under two centuries of Protestantism is here admitted! New England, once filled with converted Puritans, now bewailed for its unconverted state.

Immediately after Dr. Hall's remarks, there fell another *morceau*, which we will pluck by the way: "Mr. Moody, of Chicago," says the report, "made the noteworthy remark that city missions had proved failures, on the ground that the wrangling among the different sects prevented the creation of permanent congregations from the converts made." Whether that is the sole ground of their failure we will not discuss now, since it would be but a repetition of what has already been said. H. F. Durant, of Boston, then appealed to the ministry, "to *thunder* from the pulpits against infidelity." But suppose the writings of Theodore Parker, who is the legitimate brain-child of John Calvin, should thunder back. What then? The thoughtful mind of Boston and Massachusetts understands, and has understood for some time, which has the best of the argument.

I will not reiterate another statement I have made; it will suggest itself to your minds when I say that at that very session the Rev. Dr. Matlock said, "that there was a deal of infidelity *in the Church*. All around he saw a world of human beings going down to the blackness of death."

But let us look a little at what went on the last day of the Convention. In discussing the question, "By what means can we (the Protestants) reach those who do not come to our churches?" Mr. Moody said, among other things, "What we wanted was live preaching to reach the masses; that opera-singing in churches can't do it." So Protestantism is waking up, too, to that subordinate mistake.

Now let us see what the Rev. George Washburn said. I will not reiterate to you what I have said about Catholicity's sisterhoods and brotherhoods. It will all suggest itself to you as I read. You will remember that one of the pieces of vandalism wrought by the Continental Reformation was the abolition of Religious Orders. And some people are very much shocked indeed that our Church, true to her Catholicity, should encourage the formation of Sisterhoods of Mercy. It is considered a very alarming symptom, if not very wicked, for any woman to put on a black bonnet and habit, and devote herself to the Lord's work. But this National Protestant Convention seems to have yielded the ground to Catholicity in this matter; to have acknowledged not only that Protestantism has been guilty of a blunder, but of a very bad blunder. The subject was, "Women's work in the Church." Dr. Washburn said: "The theory that woman has no place in the Church deprives America of two-thirds of its Christian force. He would ask, was there any distinctive work for women in America? That there was, nobody would presume to deny. He then spoke of the work of women in the early Church, and of the allusions of St. Chrysostom and other Fathers to them.

The work of these holy ladies was to go out and care for the sick and poor, the widow and the orphan, and to carry the Gospel into every home and heart. Such women they wanted in connection with the Christian Church at the present day; women who would make themselves at home in every house; who would carry the precious word of life around with them, and give it a lasting tenement in the house of intemperate fathers and disconsolate wives and children, and thereby effect a complete regeneration in the morals of the wayfaring. He would again be for appointing a separate class of women for visiting jails, poor-houses, hospitals, etc., on visits of consolation and charity. The existence of charitable institutions generally through the country would be a great boon. We need trained women in the Church; we want a place where they can be educated for this field. The churches should open recruiting-offices for them. A home should also be established, so that, when our sisters return from foreign or domestic mission-work, they may find a place of welcome and of rest. Suppose we open in this city a House under the care of the Church. Here all women who desire to enlist in the service of the Lord can be trained and educated. He then alluded to the fact that the Romish Church owed two-thirds of its existence to the labors of females—the Society of St. Vincent de Paul." "Mr. McDougall highly eulogized the labors of the nuns in Canada. He said the strength of the Catholic Church lay in the sisterhoods which it had established. Their beneficent ministrations have attached all sufferers to the Church that sends them forth." "Mr. Trask, of Massachusetts, Mr. Cary, of Utica, and others spoke in high terms of approval of the object." It is to be trusted, after this flat acknowledgment of the Protestant blunder, this semi-official surrender, that this will be the last we shall hear of Puritan opposition to Sisterhoods. One more remark on the topic I cannot refrain from quoting. The Rev. Mr. Blair said, "He was glad to see so many were in favor of adopting this element of strength. The great want of Protestantism is the aid of women. We are weak"—mark that—"we are *weak* because we have *rejected* the noblest of mankind from the work Christ gave us to do."

But I must bring these rich quotations to a close. And I will do so by showing you the spirit which has pervaded Protestantism. The question was, "Why so many churches failed to reach the poor?" Several clergymen spoke in reference to the matter, "during which the question of pew-fees was extensively discussed; it being the opinion that while the rights of the poor to adequate accommodations in the church should be regarded, those of the rich should not be violated. The *general opinion* was, that proper accommodations should be secured for each, the places to be apportioned out to the poor to worship in at the smallest possible expense to them." I have only to set over against this practice of

Protestantism, thus defended, a certain remark with which some of you may be familiar. "My brethren, have not the faith of our Lord Jesus Christ with respect of persons. For if there come into your assembly a man with a gold ring, in goodly apparel, and there come in also a poor man in vile raiment, and ye have respect to him that weareth the gay clothing, and say unto him, Sit thou here in a good place; and say to the poor Stand thou there, or sit here under my footstool, are ye not then partial in yourselves and are become judges of evil thoughts? Hearken, my beloved brethren; hath not God chosen the poor of this world rich in faith and heirs of the kingdom which he hath promised to them that love Him? But ye have despised the poor." In justice be it said, there were speakers who opposed this "general opinion," and who spoke noble words of truth in reference to the subject. So there were at least marked evidences in the Convention of a reaction from another blunder of Protestantism.*

* The week after the above sermon was preached, an eminent clergyman of one of the "Collegiate Churches" of this city delivered a discourse on "The Evangelization of the Masses," in which he made the following statements, viz.: "Every age seems to have had its own peculiar problem, and certainly, from the facts with which we are familiar, this question, How shall we evangelize the masses? seems to be the one left for our solution. It has been estimated that the present population of this city is about three-fourths of a million of people, about one-half of whom are foreign born, comprising forty-two different nationalities. And for the spiritual improvement of this entire number there are about 350 churches of all denominations, capable of containing

I now come to another remarkable feature of the week. It is a leading article from one of the most prominent religious papers published in the interest of Protestantism. I select it for notice because it leads all that has been said on the other side in ability and tactics. I leave you to judge whether or not it is another practical admission

less than 325,000 people. Of evangelical churches there are 275, able to accommodate about 200,000. Of evangelical ministers there are 500, but of pastors only 250. The number of evangelical Christians is about 70,000. In other words, there are in our midst, this day, about 300,000 souls to whom the preaching of the Gospel is quite as foreign as though there were no Gospel. To obtain a conception of the vast multitude thus dead, as it were, to all Christian teaching, were they to stand side by side (allowing two feet for each), the line would not end till the twenty-seventh milestone had been passed; or were they to sit in our city cars, thirty to a car, more than 10,000 cars would be required to contain them.

"And now the question arises, How is this vast multitude to be brought under the sway of moral and Christian influence? Bibles have been profusely scattered, and pithy tracts have been systematically distributed throughout the city, and there have been established Sabbath and mission schools, prayer-meetings, sewing-societies, and reading-rooms. Various have been the instrumentalities employed to move these same multitudes, and yet no marked, deep religious impression has been made upon them. Not that the Bible and tract, the establishment of Sabbath-schools, missions, and the like, have done nothing for the evangelization of the city. By no means. But the methods which thus far have been pursued aimed at the religious improvement of the masses, as masses, have failed, inasmuch as it is undeniably true that, as a city, we are neither as moral nor as righteous as we were years ago. How, then, it is asked, is this melancholy fact to be reversed? . . . . Men may say what they may, the masses have not had the Gospel preached to them. And for the reason that the that the first campaign of the war is closed. "We can easily imagine," it says, "that some persons would think Dr. Ewer has the best of the argument *from his stand-point.* For, it seems to us, that the contest has been fought upon a false issue, which he has adroitly presented, and which his opponents have too readily allowed; that his premises involve a definition as to the aim of Protestantism which has been suffered to pass without scrutiny." So, it seems, the battle proving rather disastrous *at our stand-point*, the editor thinks it best to beat a retreat. He summons the Protestants away from the field, where they have been fighting, and tells them to mass together in another position, and there show fight, where they

missionaries, whose special work thus far this seems to have been, do not really get at the masses."

The remedy which he proposes is a more vigorous preaching of Protestantism among the masses.

Some thirty years ago, a man was taken sick with biliousness. It was in Maryland. His family physician administered calomel to him. There being no improvement, he administered the calomel in larger doses. He tried it in powders, he then tried it in pill-form; he then tried it mixed with molasses, but he failed totally in reaching the seat of the disease. At length it was resolved that a consulting physician should be called in. The two doctors retired into a room by themselves. They remained there over an hour, consulting upon the case, and then came forth and went into the sick man's room. He looked up inquiringly at them, when the consulting physician—who, by-the-way, was a man of very grave countenance—leaned over the bed, and, looking through his spectacles, said, "Mr. B——, we have thought over this case, and we would like to know *how* you would like to *take* —your calomel?"

can do better. Let us watch them as they run, and see whether it is worth our while to run after them. The writer says: "To begin with fundamentals, when is any thing proved a failure? It is when it is proved either to have ceased to exist without achieving its object, or that, if it still exists, it has not, after sufficient trial, attained the end or ends which it proposed. We trust that these positions are not questionable. Now, then, that Protestantism is a failure, because it has died without any results, will hardly be advanced."

Of course not. Protestantism has had *some* results. It has *not* failed in a good many things. It has not failed in plunging Germany into infidelity. It has not failed in keeping the poor out of churches. It has not failed in "rejecting the noblest of mankind" (viz., woman) "from the work Christ gave us to do." It has not failed, on the contrary, it has triumphantly succeeded in making Dr. Hall "bewail the unconverted state of New England." It has not failed in substituting a Sabellian God for the Tri-Unity. It has not failed in killing out all definite faith in America. It has not failed in ostracizing and mobbing those who wish to worship in a mode different from its own. But I will not go on with a list of its successes.

The writer continues: "That it still exists, will be granted by Dr. Ewer, we suppose. Therefore, if it is a failure, it is because it has not, after sufficient trial, done what it aimed at, and we allow that it has had sufficient trial, that it may be judged by its history up to this day. Thus the question is narrowed to this, What was and is the object of Protestantism? Here has been the error."

Then the writer goes on to state that it is very easy, if they permit us to define what the aim of Protestantism is, for us to make out a strong case. He says: "Thus the reverend gentleman in question has impliedly assumed that Protestantism meant the establishment of a system, or Church, or organization, which was to do certain things, and consequently urged his points as to disintegration, etc., with force, while some of his opponents tacitly admitted this idea." Exactly what that sentence means to say, I do not know, and the use of the words "and so forth" does not help to clear it much. However, whatever it is, the writer goes on to say, "But Protestantism aims at no such thing." What! Protestantism not aim at preserving Christianity on earth? Well, if it does not aim at that, it had better close its doors. Protestantism, as, forsooth, the *only* true presentment of Christianity, not aim at reaching the masses? Protestantism not aim at preserving the Bible for the world? "Oh, no!" says the writer; the enemy flee from the battle-ground. "It is merely," says the writer, "*a principle of action* asserted and assumed by certain Christians." Well, if it is frittered down to that, all we can say is, it is a worse failure than we took it to be. But, behold the enemy on the new battle-field which it has selected, and to which it has fled for safety. Protestantism has only two aims, it seems, according to the writer. They are not those that I have stated, at all. It does not care whether Christianity runs down into Rationalism or not. It does not care whether the poor have the Gospel preached unto them or not. It does not care whether or not vast regions of country, after being burned over and over again by the fires of Revivalism, are left at last dead to any religious feeling. But it seems its solitary aims are two—first, a negative aim, and second, a positive. First, "to throw off the spiritual despotism of Rome." Well, we admit that it has triumphantly succeeded in doing that. We do not deny that it has swung clear away from tyranny over to an equally disastrous license, which has wrecked its millions of souls. If that be success, then Protestantism is welcome to all the credit it can extract from it. In order for the writer to prove that, in succeeding in disenthralling herself from Roman tyranny at the same time that true Catholicity did, Protestantism did not fall into an equally bad evil, and, therefore, make a failure of it while trying to right herself, he has still got to come back to our stand-point, and drive us from our position, that Protestantism is incipient Rationalism. This we have shown to be the case, both logically and historically; and neither argument has been touched. So it is hardly worth our while, unless something more is done, to chase up the flying foe on this point.

But it seems there was one more aim of Protestantism, according to the writer. It was, "to promote the spread of the Bible and the preaching of the pure Gospel—the evangelical as distinct from the sacerdotal system"; that is to say, the preaching of Protestantism! Of course, we admit that the Protestants have succeeded marvellously in preaching Protestantism. The foe is shrewd. But his shrewdness does not save him. He is not permitted thus to dodge the question. Of course, Protestantism has succeeded in preaching Protestantism, but the real question is, what have been the effects, the results, of that Protestantism which has been preached? The real question is, whether Protestantism *is* the "pure Gospel." He assumes that. But he is not permitted thus to beg the question. We admit, too, that Protestantism has helped true Catholicity in spreading the Bible. But the real question is, what have been the effects of the peculiar mode in which Protestantism has turned the Bible out adrift in the world? So long as they yield to us the point that the effects have been bad, they are welcome to all the credit they can extract from the mere fact itself of their spreading the Bible. And it is still less worth our while to chase up the flying foe on this other point.

And now comes the best thing in this

shrewdly-written paper. It is the most excellent attempt yet at clouding the matter. He says of us: "If our points are met, that will not prove Protestantism a success; and even if they cannot be met, the reverse does not inevitably result." How does he sustain this assertion? Why, as follows: "If he (Dr. Ewer) shows that there follow upon Protestantism Rationalism and disintegration of organizations, he merely shows that men have abused the good principle of liberty of conscience (and abuse of a good thing is always possible)." Certainly, if I had simply shown that Rationalism follows as a mere fact. But the difficulty is, more has been shown than this, viz., that the inevitable *logical result* of Protestantism is Rationalism; that, if any man thinks and is unrestrained by other influences, such as prejudice, social affection, position before the world, or what not, he is bound to go down from Protestant premises to the Rationalistic conclusion; that the Unitarians decidedly have the argument on the Orthodox Congregationalists. The mere assertion that "men may have abused the good principle of liberty of conscience" does not meet this. It is not a question as to abuse of a good principle. It is a question as to whether or not thinking men can help themselves; whether they are not bound to follow premises to their legitimate conclusion. And there is no way for Protestants to escape their dilemma, but to show that Rationalism is not the logical conclusion of Protestantism. But the writer goes on: "If he (Dr. Ewer) shows that it (Prótestantism) has failed to reach the masses, the reply is not to be a *tu quoque* to Catholicism, but to admit that the zeal of Protestants has not been equal to their light, not that they could not reach the masses if they would." But the difficulty, brethren, is, we have not only shown *that* Protestantism has failed to reach the masses, but *why* it has failed, and that it is positively *not* from want of zeal. And the points we have made on this have not been touched.

Why, my friends, is it possible that what has hitherto been said on the other side is all that can be said for this great phenomenon of Protestantism? One can hardly believe his eyes as he reads what has been written. But I turn to our writer. He concludes his article as follows, viz.: "It seems that this is the true way to meet the preacher whose words have startled and shocked us, by showing that he takes a false position; and also, it seems that, to meet him thus, provides a way of turning the tables on him, on which we may dwell at another time. In closing, we hope that some one may take up and develop more at length, and accurately, this question which we have briefly sought to present—that is, what does Protestantism seek to do, and how has it succeeded therein?" The writer very prudently introduces the above paragraph with the words, "It may be we are mistaken." It is for you to decide, brethren, whether he has made out his case. One thing is evident—he is keen enough to see that the first campaign is about closed.

THE END.

www.ingramcontent.com/pod-product-compliance
Lightning Source LLC
LaVergne TN
LVHW021359110826
845150LV00007B/1712